Working Papers, Volume 2
Chapters 12-25

for use with

Fundamental Accounting Principles

Eighteenth Edition

John J. Wild
University of Wisconsin, Madison

Kermit D. Larson
University of Texas at Austin

Barbara Chiappetta
Nassau Community College

Prepared by
John J. Wild
University of Wisconsin, Madison

Boston   Burr Ridge, IL   Dubuque, IA   Madison, WI   New York   San Francisco   St. Louis
Bangkok   Bogotá   Caracas   Kuala Lumpur   Lisbon   London   Madrid   Mexico City
Milan   Montreal   New Delhi   Santiago   Seoul   Singapore   Sydney   Taipei   Toronto

Working Papers, Volume 2, Chapters 12-25 for use with
FUNDAMENTAL ACCOUNTING PRINCIPLES
John J. Wild, Kermit D. Larson, and Barbara Chiappetta

Published by McGraw-Hill, an imprint of The McGraw-Hill Companies, Inc., 1221 Avenue of the Americas,
New York, NY 10020. Copyright © 2007 by The McGraw-Hill Companies, Inc. All rights reserved.

5 6 7 8 9 0 CUS/CUS 0 9 8

ISBN 13: 978-0-07-326640-4
ISBN 10: 0-07-326640-X

Table of Contents

(a) _____
_____
_____

(b) _____
_____
_____

Quick Study 12-2

	Share to Stolton	Share to Bright	Total
Net income			
Salary allowance:			
Stolton			
Bright			
Total salary allowances			
Balance of income			
Balance allocated:			
Stolton			
Bright			
Total allocated			
Balance of income			
Shares of the partners			

Quick Study 12-3

_____
_____
_____

Quick Study 12-4

_____
_____
_____
_____

GENERAL JOURNAL

Date	Account Titles and Explanation	P. R.	Debit	Credit

Quick Study 12-6

GENERAL JOURNAL

Date	Account Titles and Explanation	P. R.	Debit	Credit

Quick Study 12-7

_____
_____
_____
_____
_____
_____
_____
_____
_____

Characteristic	General Partnerships
1. Life	
2. Owners' liability	
3. Legal status	
4. Tax status of income	
5. Owners' authority	
6. Ease of formation	
7. Transferability of ownership	
8. Ability to raise large amounts of capital	

Exercise 12-2
Part a

Recommended Organization: _____

_____
_____
_____
_____
_____

Taxation Effects: _____

_____
_____

Advantages: _____

_____
_____
_____

Recommended Organization: _____
_____
_____
_____
_____
_____

Taxation Effects: _____
_____
_____

Advantages: _____
_____
_____
_____

Part c

Recommended Organization: _____
_____
_____
_____
_____
_____

Taxation Effects: _____
_____
_____

Advantages: _____
_____
_____
_____

(1)

GENERAL JOURNAL

Date	Account Titles and Explanation	P. R.	Debit	Credit
(a)				
(b)				
(c)				

(2)

Capital account balances:	Eckert	Kelley
Initial investment		
Withdrawals		
Share of income		
Ending balances		

	Share to Kramer	Share to Knox	Total
(1)			
(2)			
(3)			

	Share to Kramer	Share to Knox	Total
(1)			
(2)			

Exercise 12-6

GENERAL JOURNAL

Date	Account Titles and Explanation	P. R.	Debit	Credit

(1)

GENERAL JOURNAL

Date	Account Titles and Explanation	P. R.	Debit	Credit

(2)

GENERAL JOURNAL

Date	Account Titles and Explanation	P. R.	Debit	Credit

(3)

GENERAL JOURNAL

Date	Account Titles and Explanation	P. R.	Debit	Credit

(1)

GENERAL JOURNAL

Date	Account Titles and Explanation	P. R.	Debit	Credit

(2)

GENERAL JOURNAL

Date	Account Titles and Explanation	P. R.	Debit	Credit

(3)

GENERAL JOURNAL

Date	Account Titles and Explanation	P. R.	Debit	Credit

(1)

	Red	White	Blue	Total
Initial investments				
Allocation of all losses				
Capital balances				

(2)

GENERAL JOURNAL

Date		Account Titles and Explanation	P. R.	Debit	Credit

(3)

GENERAL JOURNAL

Date		Account Titles and Explanation	P. R.	Debit	Credit

(a) Loss computation from selling assets:

_____
_____
_____
_____
_____
_____
_____
_____

(b) Loss allocation

	Turner	Roth	Lowe	Total
Capital balance before loss liquidation......................				
Allocation of loss:				
Capital balances after loss............				

(c) Liability to be paid:

_____
_____
_____

(a) Loss computation from selling assets: _____

_____

_____

_____

_____

_____

_____

(b) Loss and deficit allocation:

	Turner	Roth	Lowe	Total
Capital balance before loss.........				
Allocation of loss:				
Capital balances after loss............				
Allocation of _____ deficit to				
Cash paid by each partner............				

(c) Liability to be paid: _____

_____

Exercise 12-12

_____

_____

_____

_____

_____

_____

_____

_____

_____

_____

GENERAL JOURNAL

Date	Account Titles and Explanation	P. R.	Debit	Credit
(1)				
(2)				
(3)				

Supporting calculations:

_____

_____

_____

_____

_____

_____

_____

_____

_____

_____

_____

_____

_____

_____

_____

Inc./Loss Sharing Plan	Year 1 Calculations
(a)	
(b)	
(c)	
(d)	

Inc./Loss Sharing Plan	Year 2 Calculations
(a)	
(b)	
(c)	
(d)	

Inc./Loss Sharing Plan	Year 3 Calculations
(a)	
(b)	
(c)	
(d)	

Supporting Work Space:

Inc./Loss Sharing Plan	Calculations			Total
(a)				
(b)				
(c)				

				Total
PARTNERSHIP				
Statement of Partners' Equity				
For Year Ended December 31				

				Total
Beg. capital balances				
Plus:				
Owner investments				
Net Income:				
Salary allowances				
Interest allowances				
Balance allocated				
Total net income				
Total				
Less partners' withdrawals				
End. capital balances				

Part 3

GENERAL JOURNAL

Date	Account Titles and Explanation	P. R.	Debit	Credit

GENERAL JOURNAL

Date	Account Titles and Explanation	P. R.	Debit	Credit
(a)				
(b)				
(c)				
(d)				
(e)				

GENERAL JOURNAL

Date	Account Titles and Explanation	P. R.	Debit	Credit
(a)				
(b)				
(c)				

(1)

GENERAL JOURNAL

Date	Account Titles and Explanation	P. R.	Debit	Credit

GENERAL JOURNAL

Date		Account Titles and Explanation	P. R.	Debit	Credit

(3)

GENERAL JOURNAL

Date		Account Titles and Explanation	P. R.	Debit	Credit

(4)

GENERAL JOURNAL

Date		Account Titles and Explanation	P. R.	Debit	Credit

(1) _____
_____
_____
_____
_____
_____
_____

(2) _____
_____
_____
_____
_____
_____
_____
_____

(3) _____
_____
_____
_____
_____
_____

Comparative Analysis--BTN 12-2
(1) _____
_____
_____

(2) _____
_____
_____

(3) _____
_____

(4) _____
_____
_____
_____

(1) Income allocation per original agreement:

	Maben	Orlando	Clark	Total
Salary allowance				
Per patient charges				
Totals				

(2) Income allocation per Clark's proposal:

	Maben	Orlando	Clark	Total
Per patient charges				

(3)

_____

_____

_____

_____

_____

_____

_____

_____

_____

STUDY NOTES
Organizations with Partnership Characteristics

(1) _____
_____
_____
_____
_____
_____

(2) _____
_____
_____
_____

(3) _____
_____
_____
_____
_____
_____

(1)

Income/Loss Sharing Plan	Calculations	Baker	Warner	Rice	Total
(a)					
(b)					
(c)					
(d)					

(2) Team members share solutions.

(3)

(1) _____
_____
_____
_____

(2) _____
_____
_____
_____

(3) _____
_____
_____
_____

Entrepreneurial Decision--BTN 12-8

(1) _____
_____
_____
_____
_____
_____

(2) _____
_____
_____

(3) _____
_____
_____
_____

Chapter 12 Global Decision--BTN 12-9 Name ______________________

(1)

(2)

(3)

True Statements: _____

_____

_____

Quick Study 13-2

GENERAL JOURNAL

Date	Account Titles and Explanation	P. R.	Debit	Credit

Quick Study 13-3

GENERAL JOURNAL

Date	Account Titles and Explanation	P. R.	Debit	Credit

GENERAL JOURNAL

Date	Account Titles and Explanation	P. R.	Debit	Credit

Quick Study 13-5

GENERAL JOURNAL

Date	Account Titles and Explanation	P. R.	Debit	Credit

Quick Study 13-6
(1)

GENERAL JOURNAL

Date	Account Titles and Explanation	P. R.	Debit	Credit

(2)

GENERAL JOURNAL

Date		Account Titles and Explanation	P. R.	Debit	Credit

Quick Study 13-8

Jun Company
Stockholders' Equity
April 2 (after stock dividend)

_____

_____

_____

_____

_____

_____

_____

_____

_____

_____

_____

_____

_____

_____

_____

_____

Quick Study 13-9

Cash Dividend to Common Shareholders

_____

_____

_____

_____

_____

GENERAL JOURNAL

Date	Account Titles and Explanation	P. R.	Debit	Credit

Quick Study 13-11

(1) _____

_____

_____

_____

(2) _____

_____

_____

Quick Study 13-12

Basic Earnings Per Share _____

_____

_____

_____

Quick Study 13-13

Basic Earnings Per Share _____

_____

_____

_____

_____

Price-Earnings Ratio

_____
_____
_____

Analysis

_____
_____
_____
_____

Quick Study 13-15

Dividend Yield

_____
_____
_____

Analysis

_____
_____
_____
_____

Quick Study 13-16

_____
_____
_____
_____
_____
_____
_____
_____

	Characteristic	Corporations
1.	Owner authority & control	
2.	Ease of formation	
3.	Transferability of ownership	
4.	Ability to raise large amounts of capital	
5.	Duration of Life	
6.	Owner liability	
7.	Legal status	
8.	Tax status of income	

Exercise 13-2

GENERAL JOURNAL

Date	Account Titles and Explanation	P. R.	Debit	Credit
(1)				
(2)				
(3)				

GENERAL JOURNAL

Date		Account Titles and Explanation	P. R.	Debit	Credit
(1)					
(2)					
(3)					
(4)					

GENERAL JOURNAL

Date		Account Titles and Explanation	P. R.	Debit	Credit

Exercise 13-5

(1) _____   (4) _____

(2) _____   (5) _____

(3) _____   (6) _____

Part 1

(a) Retained Earnings:

_____
_____
_____
_____

(b) Total Stockholders' Equity:

_____
_____
_____
_____
_____
_____

(c) Number of Outstanding Shares:

_____
_____
_____
_____
_____

Part 2

(a) Retained Earnings:

_____
_____
_____
_____

(b) Total Stockholders' Equity:

_____
_____
_____
_____
_____

(c) Number of Outstanding Shares:

_____
_____
_____
_____

Part 3

_____
_____
_____
_____
_____

Name _____
Part 1

GENERAL JOURNAL

Date		Account Titles and Explanation	P. R.	Debit	Credit

Part 2

	Before	After

Part 3

	Feb. 5	Feb. 28

	Preferred	Common
2006:		
2007:		
2008:		
2009:		
Totals:		

Exercise 13-9

	Preferred	Common
2006:		
2007:		
2008:		
2009:		
Totals:		

GENERAL JOURNAL

Date	Account Titles and Explanation	P. R.	Debit	Credit

Changes to the equity section include: _____

_____
_____
_____
_____
_____
_____
_____
_____
_____
_____
_____
_____
_____
_____
_____
_____
_____
_____
_____
_____

Revised Stockholders' Equity Section (for support of your part 2 solution):

AMOS COMPANY
Statement of Retained Earnings
For Year Ended December 31, 2008

(1) Net Income Available to Common Stockholders: _____

_____

_____

_____

_____

_____

(2) Basic Earnings per Share: _____

_____

_____

_____

_____

_____

Exercise 13-13

(1) Net Income Available to Common Stockholders: _____

_____

_____

_____

_____

_____

(2) Basic Earnings per Share: _____

_____

_____

_____

_____

Price-Earnings Ratio:

(1) _____

(2) _____

(3) _____

(4) _____

Analysis: _____

Exercise 13-15
Dividend Yield:

(1) _____

(2) _____

(3) _____

(4) _____

Analysis: _____

Exercise 13-16

(1) _____

_____

(2) _____

Part 1

(a) _____

(b) _____

(c) _____

(d) _____

_____

Part 2

Number of Outstanding Shares: _____

_____

_____

_____

_____

Part 3

Minimum Legal Capital: _____

_____

Part 4

Total Paid-In Capital from Common Stockholders: _____

_____

_____

_____

_____

Part 5

Book Value Per Common Share: _____

_____

_____

_____

GENERAL JOURNAL

Date	Account Titles and Explanation	P. R.	Debit	Credit

_____ CORPORATION

Statement of Retained Earnings

For Year Ended December 31, 2009

Part 3

_____ CORPORATION

Stockholders' Equity Section of the Balance Sheet

December 31, 2009

Explanations for each of the entries:

Oct. 2 (Jan.17)* _____

_____

Oct 25 (Feb. 5)* _____

_____

Oct. 31 (Feb. 28)* _____

_____

Nov. 5 (Mar. 14)* _____

_____

Dec. 1(Mar. 25)* _____

_____

Dec. 31 (Mar. 31)* _____

_____

* Dates for Problem 13-3B are in parentheses.

Part 2

	Oct. 2 (Jan. 17)*	Oct. 25 (Feb. 5)*	Oct. 31 (Feb. 28)*	Nov. 5 (Mar. 14)*	Dec. 1 (Mar. 25)*	Dec. 31 (Mar. 31)*
Common stock...............						
Common stock dividend distributable...						
Paid-In capital in excess of par.............						
Retained earnings........						
Total equity.................						

*Dates for Problem 13-3B are in parentheses.

Problem 13-4A or 13-4B
Part 1

Outstanding Common Shares _____

_____

_____

_____

_____

_____

_____

_____

Cash Dividend Amounts:

_____

_____

_____

_____

_____

Part 3

Capitalization of Retained Earnings:

_____

_____

_____

_____

_____

Part 4

Cost Per Share of Treasury Stock:

_____

_____

_____

_____

_____

Part 5

Net Income Computation:

_____

_____

_____

_____

_____

_____

_____

_____

_____

(1) Market Price Per Share:

_____

_____

(2) Computation of Stock Par Values:

_____

_____

_____

_____

(3) Book Value Per Preferred Share:

_____

_____

_____

Book Value Per Common Share:

_____

_____

_____

_____

(4) Book Value Per Preferred Share:

_____

_____

_____

_____

Book Value Per Common Share:

_____

_____

_____

_____

_____

_____

_____

(5) Book Value Per Preferred Share:

_____

_____

_____

_____

_____

_____

Book Value Per Common Share:

_____

_____

_____

_____

_____

_____

_____

(6) _____

_____

_____

_____

_____

_____

_____

(7) _____

_____

_____

_____

_____

Success Systems

(1a) GENERAL JOURNAL

Date	Account Titles and Explanation	P. R.	Debit	Credit

(1b) GENERAL JOURNAL

Date	Account Titles and Explanation	P. R.	Debit	Credit

(1c) GENERAL JOURNAL

Date	Account Titles and Explanation	P. R.	Debit	Credit

(2) (a)

(b)

(c)

(3)

(1) _____

_____

_____

_____

_____

_____

_____

_____

(2) _____

_____

_____

_____

_____

_____

(3) _____

_____

_____

_____

(4) _____

_____

_____

_____

_____

(5) _____

_____

_____

(6) Fast Forward: _____

_____

_____

_____

_____

(1)
Best Buy Book Value Per Common Share:
_____
_____
_____

Circuit City Book Value Per Common Share:
_____
_____
_____

(2)
Best Buy Earnings Per Share:
_____
_____
_____

Circuit City Earnings per Share:
_____
_____
_____
_____
_____

(3)
Best Buy Dividend Yield:
_____
_____
_____

Circuit City Dividend Yield:
_____
_____
_____

Analysis:
_____
_____
_____

(4)
Best Buy Price-Earnings Ratio:
_____
_____
_____

Circuit City Price-Earnings Ratio:
_____
_____
_____

Analysis & Interpretation:
_____
_____
_____
_____

_____
_____
_____
_____
_____
_____
_____
_____
_____
_____
_____
_____
_____
_____
_____
_____
_____
_____
_____
_____
_____
_____
_____
_____
_____
_____
_____
_____
_____
_____
_____
_____

MEMORANDUM

TO:
FROM:
DATE:
SUBJECT:

Company	Earnings Per Share	Market Price of Stock	Price-Earnings Ratio

Industry Norm:

Meaning of Price-Earnings Ratio:

Comparison Across Companies:

Concluding Analysis:

Chapter 13 Taking It to the Net Name ______________________

Part 1 BTN 13-5

Part 2

Part 3

Part 4

Part 1
(a) Impact on Financial Position due to Stock Buyback: _____
_____
_____
_____
_____
_____
_____

(b) Reasons for Stock Buyback: _____
_____
_____
_____
_____
_____
_____
_____

GENERAL JOURNAL

Date	Account Titles and Explanation	P. R.	Debit	Credit
Reacquisition entry				
(a)				
(b)				
(c)				
(d)				
(e)				

Part 3

Similarities: _____

_____

_____

Differences: _____

_____

_____

(1) _____

_____

_____

_____

_____

(2) _____

_____

_____

_____

_____

(3) _____

_____

_____

_____

_____

_____

	Plan A	Plan B

Part 2

	Plan A	Plan B

Part 3

_____

_____

_____

_____

_____

_____

_____

_____

Global Decision--BTN 13-10

(1) Book Value per Common Share _____

_____

_____

_____

_____

(2) Earnings per Share _____

_____

_____

_____

_____

(3) Analysis _____

_____

_____

_____

_____

_____

(1) Cash Proceeds: _____
_____

(2) Total Bond Interest Expense: _____
_____
_____
_____
_____

(3) Bond Interest Expense on 1st Payment Date: _____
_____
_____

Quick Study 14-2[B]

(1) Cash Proceeds: _____
_____

(2) Total Bond Interest Expense: _____
_____
_____
_____
_____

(3) Bond Interest Expense on 1st Payment Date: _____
_____
_____

GENERAL JOURNAL

Date		Account Titles and Explanation	P. R.	Debit	Credit

Quick Study 14-4

(a) _____

_____

_____

_____

_____

_____

_____

_____

_____

(b) _____

_____

_____

_____

_____

_____

_____

GENERAL JOURNAL

Date	Account Titles and Explanation	P. R.	Debit	Credit

Quick Study 14-6

GENERAL JOURNAL

Date	Account Titles and Explanation	P. R.	Debit	Credit

(a) _____

_____

_____

(b) _____

_____

_____

(c) _____

_____

_____

Quick Study 14-8

1. _____ Registered bond		5. _____ Convertible bond
2 _____ Serial bond		6. _____ Bond indenture
3. _____ Secured bond		7. _____ Sinking fund bond
4. _____ Bearer bond		8. _____ Debenture

Quick Study 14-9

Ratio Computations: _____

_____

_____

_____

_____

_____

_____

Analysis and Interpretation: _____

_____

_____

_____

_____

GENERAL JOURNAL

Date	Account Titles and Explanation	P. R.	Debit	Credit

Quick Study 14-11^D

GENERAL JOURNAL

Date	Account Titles and Explanation	P. R.	Debit	Credit

Quick Study 14-12^D

GENERAL JOURNAL

Date	Account Titles and Explanation	P. R.	Debit	Credit

(1) _____

_____

_____

_____

(2)

GENERAL JOURNAL

	Date	Account Titles and Explanation	P. R.	Debit	Credit
(a)					
(b)					
(c)					

(3)

GENERAL JOURNAL

	Date	Account Titles and Explanation	P. R.	Debit	Credit
(a)					
(b)					

(1) _____

_____

_____

_____

(2) Total Bond Interest Expense: _____

_____

_____

_____

_____

_____

_____

_____

(3)

Semiannual Period-End	Unamortized Discount	Carrying Value
1/01/2008		
6/30/2008		
12/31/2008		
6/30/2009		
12/31/2009		
6/30/2010		
12/31/2010		

(1) _____

_____

_____

_____

(2) Total Bond Interest Expense:

_____

_____

_____

_____

_____

_____

_____

_____

_____

_____

_____

(3)

Semiannual Interest Period-End	(A) Cash Interest Paid (4.5% x $500,000)	(B) Bond Interest Expense [6% x Prior (E)]	(C) Discount Amortization [(B) - (A)]	(D) Unamortized Discount [Prior (D) - (C)]	(E) Carrying Value [$500,000-(D)]
1/01/2008					
6/30/2008					
12/31/2008					
6/30/2009					
12/31/2009					
6/30/2010					
12/31/2010					

(1) _____

_____

_____

_____

(2) Total Bond Interest Expense:

_____

_____

_____

_____

_____

_____

_____

_____

_____

(3)

Semiannual Period-End	Unamortized Premium	Carrying Value
1/01/2008		
6/30/2008		
12/31/2008		
6/30/2009		
12/31/2009		
6/30/2010		
12/31/2010		

(1) _____

_____

_____

(2) Total Bond Interest Expense:

_____

_____

_____

_____

_____

_____

_____

_____

_____

_____

(3)

Semiannual Interest Period-End	(A) Cash Interest Paid [6.5% x $400,000]	(B) Bond Interest Expense [6% x Prior (E)]	(C) Premium Amortization [(A) - (B)]	(D) Unamortized Premium [Prior (D) - (C)]	(E) Carrying Value [$400,000+(D)]
1/01/2008					
6/30/2008					
12/31/2008					
6/30/2009					
12/31/2009					
6/30/2010					
12/31/2010					

(1) Semiannual Cash Interest Payment: _____

_____

_____

(2) Number of Payments: _____

_____

(3) _____

_____

(4) Market Price Computation: _____

_____

_____

_____

_____

_____

_____

(5)

GENERAL JOURNAL

Date	Account Titles and Explanation	P. R.	Debit	Credit

(1) Semiannual Cash Interest Payment:

_____

_____

_____

(2) Number of Payments:

_____

_____

_____

(3) _____

_____

_____

(4) Market Price Computation:

_____

_____

_____

_____

_____

_____

_____

(5)

GENERAL JOURNAL

Date	Account Titles and Explanation	P. R.	Debit	Credit

(1) Cash proceeds from sale:

_____
_____
_____

(2) Discount at issuance:

_____
_____
_____

(3) Total Amortization for First 6 Years:

_____
_____
_____
_____

(4) Carrying value of the bonds at 12/31/2012:

_____
_____
_____
_____
_____
_____

(5) Purchase price:

_____
_____

(6) Loss on retirement:

_____
_____
_____

(7)   **GENERAL JOURNAL**

Date		Account Titles and Explanation	P. R.	Debit	Credit

Exercise 14-9[c]

(1) _____

_____

_____

_____

_____

(2)   **GENERAL JOURNAL**

Date		Account Titles and Explanation	P. R.	Debit	Credit

(1)

Semiannual Period-End	Unamortized Discount	Carrying Value
6/01/2007		
11/30/2007		
5/31/2008		
11/30/2008		
5/31/2009		
11/30/2009		
5/31/2010		
11/30/2010		
5/31/2011		

Supporting computations:

_____
_____
_____
_____
_____
_____
_____
_____
_____
_____

Date	Account Titles and Explanation	P. R.	Debit	Credit

(1) Amount of Each Payment: _____

_____

_____

_____

(2)

Period Ending Date	(A) Beginning Balance [Prior (E)]	(B) Debit Interest Expense [7% x (A)]	+	(C) Debit Notes Payable [(D) - (B)]	=	(D) Credit Cash [computed]	(E) Ending Balance [(A) - (C)]
			Payments				
2008							
2009							
2010							
2011							

GENERAL JOURNAL

Date	Account Titles and Explanation	P. R.	Debit	Credit

(1)(a) _____

_____

_____

_____

   (b) _____

_____

_____

_____

(2) _____

_____

_____

_____

_____

_____

_____

_____

_____

(1) _____
(2) _____
(3) _____

Exercise 14-15^D

GENERAL JOURNAL

Date	Account Titles and Explanation	P. R.	Debit	Credit
(1)				
(2)				

Exercise 14-16^D

_____
_____
_____
_____
_____
_____
_____
_____
_____
_____
_____

Part 1

(a)

Cash Flow	PV Table Value	Amount	Present Value

(b)

GENERAL JOURNAL

Date		Account Titles and Explanation	P. R.	Debit	Credit

Part 2

(a)

Cash Flow	PV Table Value	Amount	Present Value

(b)

GENERAL JOURNAL

Date		Account Titles and Explanation	P. R.	Debit	Credit

(a)

Cash Flow	PV Table Value	Amount	Present Value

(b)

GENERAL JOURNAL

Date	Account Titles and Explanation	P. R.	Debit	Credit

Problem 14-2A or 14-2B
Part 1

GENERAL JOURNAL

Date	Account Titles and Explanation	P. R.	Debit	Credit

(a) Cash Payment: _____
_____
_____

(b) Semiannual Amortization: _____
_____
_____

(c) Bond Interest Expense: _____
_____
_____

Part 3

Total Bond Interest Expense: _____
_____
_____
_____
_____
_____
_____
_____
_____

Part 4

Semiannual Period-End	Unamortized Discount	Carrying Value
1/01/2007		
6/30/2007		
12/31/2007		
6/30/2008		
12/31/2008		

GENERAL JOURNAL

Date	Account Titles and Explanation	P. R.	Debit	Credit

Part 6--Requirements 1 through 5 are repeated assuming a bond premium

Requirement 1

GENERAL JOURNAL

Date	Account Titles and Explanation	P. R.	Debit	Credit

Requirement 2

(a) Cash Payment: _____

_____

(b) Semiannual Amortization: _____

_____

_____

(c) Bond Interest Expense: _____

_____

_____

Requirement 3

Total Bond Interest Expense:

_____
_____
_____
_____
_____
_____
_____
_____
_____

Requirement 4

Semiannual Period-End	Unamortized Premium	Carrying Value
1/01/2007		
6/30/2007		
12/31/2007		
6/30/2008		
12/31/2008		

Requirement 5

GENERAL JOURNAL

Date		Account Titles and Explanation	P. R.	Debit	Credit

Total Bond Interest Expense: _____

_____

_____

_____

_____

_____

_____

_____

_____

_____

Part 2

Semiannual Interest Period-End	Unamortized Premium	Carrying Value
1/01/2007		
6/30/2007		
12/31/2007		
6/30/2008		
12/31/2008		
6/30/2009		
12/31/2009		
6/30/2010		
12/31/2010		
6/30/2011		
12/31/2011		

GENERAL JOURNAL

Date	Account Titles and Explanation	P. R.	Debit	Credit

Total Bond Interest Expense: _____

_____
_____
_____
_____
_____
_____
_____
_____

Part 2

Semiannual Interest Period-End	(A) Cash Interest Paid [% x $]	(B) Bond Interest Expense [% x Prior (E)]	(C) Premium Amortization [(A) - (B)]	(D) Unamortized Premium [Prior (D) - (C)]	(E) Carrying Value [$____ + (D)]
1/01/2007					
6/30/2007					
12/31/2007					
6/30/2008					
12/31/2008					
6/30/2009					
12/31/2009					
6/30/2010					
12/31/2010					
6/30/2011					
12/31/2011					

GENERAL JOURNAL

Date			P. R.	Debit	Credit

Part 4

Cash Flow	PV Table	PV Table Value	Amount	Present Value

Comparison to Part 2 Table:

_____
_____
_____
_____
_____
_____
_____
_____

Part 1

GENERAL JOURNAL

Date		Account Titles and Explanation	P. R.	Debit	Credit

Part 2

Total Bond Interest Expense: _____

_____

_____

_____

_____

_____

_____

_____

_____

_____

Part 3

Semiannual Interest Period-End	Unamortized Discount	Carrying Value
1/01/2007		
6/30/2007		
12/31/2007		
6/30/2008		
12/31/2008		

GENERAL JOURNAL

Date		Account Titles and Explanation	P. R.	Debit	Credit

Part 5 (for Problem 14-5A only)

_____
_____
_____
_____
_____
_____
_____
_____
_____
_____
_____
_____
_____
_____
_____
_____
_____
_____
_____

GENERAL JOURNAL

Date		Account Titles and Explanation	P. R.	Debit	Credit

Part 2

Total Bond Interest Expense: _____

_____

_____

_____

_____

_____

_____

_____

_____

_____

Part 3

Semiannual Interest Period-End	(A) Cash Interest Paid [_% x $___]	(B) Bond Interest Expense [_% x Prior (E)]	(C) Discount Amortization [(B) - (A)]	(D) Unamortized Discount [Prior (D) - (C)]	(E) Carrying Value [$____ - (D)]
1/01/2007					
6/30/2007					
12/31/2007					
6/30/2008					
12/31/2008					

GENERAL JOURNAL

Date		Account Titles and Explanation	P. R.	Debit	Credit

Part 1

GENERAL JOURNAL

Date		Account Titles and Explanation	P. R.	Debit	Credit

Part 2

Total Bond Interest Expense: _____

_____

_____

_____

_____

_____

_____

_____

_____

Part 3

Semiannual Interest Period-End	(A) Cash Interest Paid [_% x $___]	(B) Bond Interest Expense [_% x Prior (E)]	(C) Premium Amortization [(A) - (B)]	(D) Unamortized Premium [Prior (D) - (C)]	(E) Carrying Value [$___ + (D)]
1/01/2007					
6/30/2007					
12/31/2007					
6/30/2008					
12/31/2008					

Chapter 14   Problem 14-7A^B or 14-7B^B Name _____

Part 4

GENERAL JOURNAL

Date	Account Titles and Explanation	P. R.	Debit	Credit

Part 5

GENERAL JOURNAL

Date	Account Titles and Explanation	P. R.	Debit	Credit

Part 6

_____
_____
_____
_____
_____
_____
_____
_____
_____
_____
_____
_____
_____

Amount of Each Payment: _____

_____
_____
_____
_____
_____
_____
_____
_____
_____

Part 2

		Payments			
	(A)	(B)	(C)	(D)	(E)
		Debit	Debit		
Period	Beginning	Interest	Notes	Credit	Ending
Ending	Balance	Expense +	Payable =	Cash	Balance
Date	[Prior (E)]	[____% x (A)]	[(D) - (B)]	[computed]	[(A) - (C)]

GENERAL JOURNAL

Date	Account Titles and Explanation	P. R.	Debit	Credit

_____ Company Ratio: _____

_____

_____

_____

_____

_____

_____ Company Ratio: _____

_____

_____

_____

_____

Part 2

Analysis and Interpretation: _____

_____

_____

_____

_____

_____

_____

_____

_____

Part 1

Present Value of the Lease Payments:

_____

_____

_____

_____

Part 2

GENERAL JOURNAL

Date	Account Titles and Explanation	P. R.	Debit	Credit

Part 3

Capital Lease Liability Payment (Amortization) Schedule:

Period Ending Date	Beginning Balance of Lease Liability	Interest on Lease Liability (__%)	Reduction of Lease Liability	Cash Lease Payment	Ending Balance of Lease Liability
Year 1					
Year 2					
Year 3					
Year 4					
Year 5					

Part 4

GENERAL JOURNAL

Date	Account Titles and Explanation	Ref.	Debit	Credit

Part 1
Maximum Loan Allowed: _____

_____
_____
_____
_____
_____
_____
_____
_____
_____
_____
_____

Part 2
(a) Percent of Assets Financed by Debt _____

_____
_____
_____

(b) Percent of Assets Financed by Equity _____

_____
_____
_____

Part 3 _____

_____
_____
_____
_____

(1) _____

_____

_____

_____

_____

_____

_____

_____

_____

(2) _____

_____

_____

(3) _____

_____

_____

(4) Fast Forward: _____

_____

_____

_____

_____

_____

_____

_____

_____

(1) Best Buy

      Current Year: _____

_____

_____

_____

_____

      Prior Year: _____

_____

_____

_____

Circuit City

      Current Year: _____

_____

_____

_____

      Prior Year: _____

_____

_____

_____

(2) _____

_____

_____

_____

_____

_____

(1) _____
_____
_____
_____
_____
_____
_____
_____
_____
_____
_____
_____

(2) _____
_____
_____
_____
_____
_____
_____
_____
_____

MEMORANDUM

TO:
FROM:
DATE:
SUBJECT:

_____
_____
_____
_____
_____
_____
_____
_____
_____
_____
_____
_____
_____
_____
_____
_____
_____
_____
_____
_____
_____
_____
_____
_____
_____
_____
_____
_____
_____
_____
_____
_____
_____
_____

(1) Long Term Liabilities: _____

_____

_____

_____

_____

_____

_____

(2a) _____

_____

_____

_____

_____

_____

(2b) _____

_____

_____

_____

_____

_____

_____
_____
_____
_____
_____
_____
_____
_____
_____
_____
_____
_____
_____
_____
_____
_____
_____
_____
_____

Part 3

_____
_____
_____
_____
_____
_____
_____
_____

Part 4

_____
_____
_____
_____
_____
_____

Similarities	Differences

Part 2

Part 3

Part 4

	Current	Alternative Notes for Expansion				
		10% Note	15% Note	16% Note	17% Note	20% Note
Income before interest............						
interest............						
Net income.......						
Equity..............						
Return on equity..						

Work Space:

_____

_____

_____

Part 2

_____

_____

_____

_____

_____

_____

_____

_____

_____

_____

_____
_____
_____
_____
_____
_____
_____
_____
_____
_____

Global Decision--BTN 14-10

(1) Dixon's Current Year Ratio: _____
_____
_____
_____

Dixon's Prior Year Ratio: _____
_____
_____
_____
_____

(2) _____
_____
_____
_____
_____

GENERAL JOURNAL

Date	Account Titles and Explanation	P. R.	Debit	Credit

Quick Study 15-2

(1)   GENERAL JOURNAL

Date	Account Titles and Explanation	P. R.	Debit	Credit

(2)

_____

_____

_____

_____

_____

(3)   GENERAL JOURNAL

Date	Account Titles and Explanation	P. R.	Debit	Credit

GENERAL JOURNAL

Date	Account Titles and Explanation	P. R.	Debit	Credit

Quick Study 15-4

GENERAL JOURNAL

Date	Account Titles and Explanation	P. R.	Debit	Credit

True: _____
_____
_____

Quick Study 15-6

(1) _____   (4) _____
(2) _____   (5) _____
(3) _____

Quick Study 15-7

GENERAL JOURNAL

Date	Account Titles and Explanation	P. R.	Debit	Credit

Quick Study 15-8

GENERAL JOURNAL

Date	Account Titles and Explanation	P. R.	Debit	Credit

GENERAL JOURNAL

Date		Account Titles and Explanation	P. R.	Debit	Credit

Quick Study 15-10

(1)

GENERAL JOURNAL

Date		Account Titles and Explanation	P. R.	Debit	Credit

(2) _____

_____

_____

_____

_____

_____

_____
_____
_____
_____
_____
_____

Quick Study 15-12

_____
_____
_____
_____
_____
_____
_____
_____

GENERAL JOURNAL

Date	Account Titles and Explanation	P. R.	Debit	Credit
	Date of Sale:			
	Date of Payment:			

Quick Study 15-14^A

GENERAL JOURNAL

Date	Account Titles and Explanation	P. R.	Debit	Credit

GENERAL JOURNAL

Date	Account Titles and Explanation	P. R.	Debit	Credit

(1)   GENERAL JOURNAL

Date	Account Titles and Explanation	P. R.	Debit	Credit

(2) _____

_____

_____

_____

_____

(3)   GENERAL JOURNAL

Date	Account Titles and Explanation	P. R.	Debit	Credit

Exercise 15-3

Available-for-Sale Portfolio	Cost	Market	Unrealized Gain (Loss)

GENERAL JOURNAL

Date	Account Titles and Explanation	P. R.	Debit	Credit

GENERAL JOURNAL

Date	Account Titles and Explanation	P. R.	Debit	Credit

GENERAL JOURNAL

Date		Account Titles and Explanation	P. R.	Debit	Credit

Computation of Market Adjustment:

Securities	Cost	Market	Unrealized Gain (Loss)

Exercise 15-6

GENERAL JOURNAL

Date		Account Titles and Explanation	P. R.	Debit	Credit

Computation of Market Adjustment:

	12/31/2007	12/31/2008
Cost		
Market		
Gain (Loss)		

GENERAL JOURNAL

Date	Account Titles and Explanation	P. R.	Debit	Credit
2006:				
2007:				
2008:				
2009:				

Supporting Computations:

(1) Classification of Investment

(a)

(b)

(c)

(d)

(e)

(2)   GENERAL JOURNAL

Date	Account Titles and Explanation	P. R.	Debit	Credit

Computation of Market Adjustment:

Long-Term AFS Securities	Cost	Market

GENERAL JOURNAL

Date	Account Titles and Explanation	P. R.	Debit	Credit
2008:				
2009:				

2008 Return on Total Assets: _____

_____

_____

_____

2009 Return on Total Assets: _____

_____

_____

_____

Analysis and Interpretation: _____

_____

_____

_____

_____

_____

_____

_____

GENERAL JOURNAL

Date		Account Titles and Explanation	P. R.	Debit	Credit
2008:					
2009:					

Reported on Quarterly Statement Ended June 30, 2008:

_____
_____
_____
_____
_____

Reported on Quarterly Statement Ended September 30, 2008:

_____
_____
_____
_____
_____

Reported on Quarterly Statement Ended December 31, 2008:

_____
_____
_____
_____
_____

Reported on Quarterly Statement Ended March 31, 2009:

_____
_____
_____
_____
_____

GENERAL JOURNAL

Date	Account Titles and Explanation	P. R.	Debit	Credit
2008:				
2009:				

GENERAL JOURNAL

Date	Account Titles and Explanation	P. R.	Debit	Credit
2010:				

Part 2

Date	Account Titles and Explanation	P. R.	Debit	Credit
2010:				

Part 1   GENERAL JOURNAL

Date	Account Titles and Explanation	P. R.	Debit	Credit

Comparison of Cost and Market Values for AFS Portfolio				
Security	Computations	Cost	Market	Unrealized Gain (Loss)

Part 3

GENERAL JOURNAL

Date	Account Titles and Explanation	P. R.	Debit	Credit

Part 4

Part 5
Income Statement:

Balance Sheet (Equity Section):

GENERAL JOURNAL

Date	Account Titles and Explanation	P. R.	Debit	Credit
2008:				

Supporting work:

GENERAL JOURNAL

Date	Account Titles and Explanation	P. R.	Debit	Credit
2009:				

Supporting work:

GENERAL JOURNAL

Date	Account Titles and Explanation	P. R.	Debit	Credit
2010:				

Supporting work:

	12/31/2008	12/31/2009	12/31/2010
Long-Term AFS Securities (cost)			
Market Adjustment			
Long-Term AFS Securities (market)			

Part 3

	2008	2009	2010
Realized Gains (Losses)			

Unrealized Gains (Losses) at year-end*

Problem 15-4A or 15-4B
Part 1
Balance sheet disclosure:

Supporting work:

AFS Securities on Dec. 31, 2008	Cost	Market

GENERAL JOURNAL

Date	Account Titles and Explanation	P. R.	Debit	Credit

Supporting Computations:

AFS Securities	Cost	Market

Part 3
Disclosures:

_____

Stock Sold	Cost	Sale Price	Realized Gain (Loss)

GENERAL JOURNAL

Date	Account Titles and Explanation	P. R.	Debit	Credit
2008:				
2009:				
2010:				

(2) Carrying Value Per Share: _____

_____

_____

_____

_____

(3) Change in Equity: _____

_____

_____

_____

_____

_____

_____

(1)

GENERAL JOURNAL

Date	Account Titles and Explanation	P. R.	Debit	Credit
2008:				
2009:				
2010:				

(2) Investment Cost Per Share: _____

_____

_____

_____

_____

(3) Change in Equity: _____

_____

_____

_____

_____

_____

_____

GENERAL JOURNAL

Date	Account Titles and Explanation	P. R.	Debit	Credit
2008:				

GENERAL JOURNAL

Date	Account Titles and Explanation	P. R.	Debit	Credit
2009:				

Part 2

Foreign Exchange Gain (Loss) Reported: _____

_____

_____

_____

_____

_____

Part 3

_____

_____

_____

_____

_____

_____

_____

_____

_____

_____

Part 1

GENERAL JOURNAL

Date	Account Titles and Explanation	P. R.	Debit	Credit

Part 2

GENERAL JOURNAL

Date	Account Titles and Explanation	P. R.	Debit	Credit

(1) _____
_____
_____

(2) _____
_____
_____
_____

(3) _____
_____
_____

(4) _____
_____
_____

(5) Fast Forward: _____
_____
_____
_____
_____
_____
_____
_____

(1) Best Buy's Return on Total Assets:

Current Year

_____

_____

Prior Year

_____

_____

Circuit City's Return on Total Assets:

Current Year

_____

_____

Prior Year

_____

_____

(2) Best Buy's Component Analysis of Return on Total Assets:

Current Year

_____

_____

Prior Year

_____

_____

_____

Circuit City's Component Analysis of Return on Total Assets:

Current Year

_____

_____

Prior Year

_____

_____

(3) Current Year Analysis:

_____

_____

Prior Year Analysis::

_____

_____

_____

_____

Name _____

(1) _____
_____
_____
_____
_____
_____
_____

(2) _____
_____
_____
_____
_____
_____
_____
_____
_____
_____
_____

(3) _____
_____
_____
_____
_____

MEMORANDUM

TO:
FROM:
DATE:
SUBJECT:

(1) _____
_____
_____
_____
_____
_____
_____

(2) _____
_____
_____
_____
_____
_____

(3) _____
_____
_____
_____
_____
_____

(4) _____
_____
_____

(1) _____

_____

_____

_____

_____

(2) _____

_____

_____

_____

_____

_____

(3) (a) _____

_____

   (b) _____

_____

   (c) _____

(4) _____

_____

_____

_____

_____

_____

(5) _____

_____

_____

_____

_____

(1) _____

GENERAL JOURNAL

Date	Account Titles and Explanation	P. R.	Debit	Credit

(2) _____

GENERAL JOURNAL

Date	Account Titles and Explanation	P. R.	Debit	Credit

(3) _____

_____

_____

Hitting the Road--BTN 15-9[A]

(1) _____

(2) _____

(3) _____

(1)   Return on Total Assets:

Current Year

_____

_____

Prior Year

_____

_____

Component Analysis of Return on Total Assets:

Current Year

_____

_____

_____

Prior Year

_____

_____

_____

(2) Current Year Analysis:

_____

_____

Prior Year Analysis:

_____

_____

_____

Overall:

_____

_____

_____

(1) _____

_____

_____

_____

(2) _____

_____

_____

_____

(3) _____

_____

_____

_____

(4) _____

_____

_____

_____

Quick Study 16-2

(1) _____	**(6)** _____
(2) _____	**(7)** _____
(3) _____	**(8)** _____
(4) _____	**(9)** _____
(5) _____	**(10)** _____

Quick Study 16-3

_____

_____

_____

_____

_____

_____

_____

_____

_____
_____
_____
_____
_____
_____
_____
_____
_____

Quick Study 16-5

(1) _____
_____
_____
_____

(2) _____
_____
_____
_____
_____
_____
_____

Quick Study 16-6

Cash Flow from Operating Activities _____
_____
_____
_____
_____
_____
_____
_____
_____

Cash Inflow from Asset Sale: _____

_____

_____

_____

_____

_____

_____

_____

Quick Study 16-8

(1) Cash Paid for Dividends _____

_____

_____

_____

_____

(2) Cash Payments toward Notes: _____

_____

_____

_____

_____

_____

Quick Study 16-9[B]

(1) Cash Received from Customer Sales: _____

_____

_____

_____

(2) Net Increase or Decrease in Cash: _____

_____

_____

_____

_____

(1) Cash Paid for Merchandise: _____

_____

_____

_____

(2) Cash Paid for Operating Expenses: _____

_____

_____

_____

Quick Study 16-11^B

Cash Flow from Operating Activities _____

_____

_____

_____

_____

_____

_____

_____

_____

_____

Quick Study 16-12

(1) _____

_____

_____

_____

_____

_____

(2) _____

_____

_____

_____

_____
_____
_____
_____
_____
_____
_____
_____

Exercise 16-1

Cash Flow from Operating Activities

_____
_____
_____
_____
_____
_____
_____
_____
_____
_____
_____

		Statement of Cash Flows			Noncash Investing & Financing Activities	Not Reported on Statement or in Note
		Operating Activities	Investing Activities	Financing Activities		
a.	Paid cash to purchase inventory.					
b.	Purchased land by issuing stock.					
c.	Accounts receivable decreased this year.					
d.	Sold equipment for cash, yielding a loss.					
e.	Recorded depreciation expense.					
f.	Income taxes payable increased this year.					
g.	Declared and paid a cash dividend.					
h.	Accounts payable decreased this year.					
i.	Paid cash to settle bond payable.					
j.	Prepaid expenses increased this year.					

		Statement of Cash Flows		Noncash Investing & Financing Activities	Not Reported on Statement or in Note
		Operating Activities	Investing Activities	Financing Activities	
a.	Retired long-term bonds payable by issuing stock.				
b.	Depreciation expense recorded.				
c.	Paid cash dividend that was declared in a prior period				
d.	Sold inventory for cash.				
e.	Borrowed cash from bank by signing a 9-month note payable.				
f.	Paid cash to purchase patent.				
g.	Accepted six-month note receivable is in exchange for plant assets.				
h.	Paid cash toward accounts payable.				
i.	Collected cash from sales.				
j.	Paid cash to acquire treasury stock.				

Cash Flows from Operating Activities

Exercise 16-5[B]

Case A

Case B

Case C

Cash Flows from Operating Activities

_____
_____
_____
_____
_____
_____
_____
_____
_____
_____
_____

<u>Supporting computations:</u>

Exercise 16-7^B

Cash Flows from Operating Activities

_____
_____
_____
_____
_____
_____
_____
_____

<u>Supporting computations:</u>

Cash Flows from Investing Activities

_____

_____

_____

_____

_____

_____

_____

Exercise 16-9

Cash Flows from Financing Activities

_____

_____

_____

_____

_____

_____

_____

Ikiban, Inc.
Statement of Cash Flows (Indirect Method)
For Year Ended June 30, 2008

Supporting Computations for:

(1) Cash received from sale of equipment:

Cash paid for new equipment:

(2) Cash paid to retire notes: _____
_____
_____

(3) Cash paid for dividends: _____
_____
_____

Part 2

Cash Flow on Total Assets Ratio: _____
_____
_____

Interpretation: _____
_____
_____

Ikiban, Inc.
Statement of Cash Flows (Direct Method)
For Year Ended June 30, 2008

<u>Supporting Computations for:</u>
(1) Cash received from customers:

(2) Cash paid for merchandise inventory:

(3) Cash paid for other operating expenses: _____

_____

_____

_____

(4) Cash paid for income taxes: _____

_____

_____

(5) Cash received from sale of equipment: _____

_____

_____

_____

Cash paid for new equipment: _____

_____

_____

_____

(6) Cash paid to retire notes: _____

_____

_____

(7) Cash paid for dividends: _____

_____

_____

_____

FERRON COMPANY
Statement of Cash Flows
For Year Ended December 31, 2008

Footnotes:

THOMAS CORPORATION
Statement of Cash Flows
For Year Ended December 31, 2008

Part 2

(a) _____

(b) _____

(c) _____

(d) _____

Statement of Cash Flows
For Year Ended December 31, 2008

Footnotes:

Supporting calculations:

_____
_____
_____
_____
_____
_____
_____
_____
_____
_____

		Analysis of changes		
	Dec. 31, 2007	Debit	Credit	Dec. 31, 2008
Balance sheet-debits:				
Cash..				
Accounts receivable.........................				
Merchandise inventory....................				
Prepaid expenses............................				
Equipment......................................				
Balance sheet-credits:				
Accum. depreciation-Equip........				
Accounts payable.....................				
Short-term notes payable..........				
Long-term notes payable...........				
Common Stock, $___par value...				
Paid-in capital in excess of				
par value, common stock........				
Retained earnings...................				
Statement of cash flows:				
Operating activities				
Net income................................				
_____ in accts. receivable...				
_____ in merch. inventory...				
_____ in prepaid expenses...				
_____ in accounts payable...				
Depreciation expense................				
_____ on sale of equipment..				
Investing activities				
Receipt from sale of equipment...				
Payment to purchase equipment..				
Financing activities				
Borrowed on short-term note....				
Payment on long-term note......				
Issued common stock for cash..				
Payments of cash dividends.....				
Noncash investing and financing activities				
Purchase of equip. financed				
by long-term note payable.....				

Spreadsheet for Statement of Cash Flows
For Year Ended December 31, 2008

Statement of Cash Flows
For Year Ended December 31, 2008

Footnotes:

Supporting calculations:

Statement of Cash Flows
For Year Ended December 31, 2008

Supporting calculations:

Spreadsheet for Statement of Cash Flows
For Year Ended December 31, 2008

	Dec. 31, 2007	Analysis of changes Debit	Credit	Dec. 31, 2008
Balance sheet-debits:				
Cash..				
Accounts receivable...........................				
Merchandise inventory......................				
Equipment......................................				
Balance sheet-credits:				
Accum. depreciation-Equip.................				
Accounts payable.............................				
Income taxes payable.......................				
Common stock, $___par value...........				
Paid-in capital in excess of				
par value, common stock............				
Retained earnings..				
Statement of cash flows:				
Operating activities				
Net income......................................				
_____ in accts. receivable..........				
_____ in merch. inventory..........				
_____ in accounts payable.........				
_____ in income taxes payable...				
Depreciation expense.....................				
Investing activities				
Payment for equipment.....................				
Financing activities				
Issued common stock for cash..........				
Paid cash dividends..........................				

Statement of Cash Flows
For Year Ended December 31, 2008

Supporting calculations:

SUCCESS SYSTEMS
Statement of Cash Flows
For Three Months Ended March 31, 2008

Supporting calculations:

(1) _____

_____

(2) _____

_____

_____

_____

(3) _____

_____

_____

_____

_____

_____

_____

_____

_____

(4) _____

_____

_____

_____

_____

_____

_____

_____

(5) Fast Forward: _____

_____

_____

_____

_____

_____

_____

_____

_____

_____

(1)   Best Buy's Cash Flow on Total Assets Ratio:
          Current Year
_____
_____
_____

          Prior Year
_____
_____
_____

      Circuit City's Cash Flow on Total Assets Ratio:
          Current Year
_____
_____
_____

          Prior Year
_____
_____
_____

(2) _____
_____
_____
_____
_____
_____

(3) _____
_____
_____
_____
_____
_____

(4) _____
_____
_____
_____
_____
_____

(1) (a) _____

_____

_____

_____

(b) _____

_____

_____

_____

_____

_____

_____

(2) _____

_____

_____

_____

_____

_____

_____

_____

_____

_____

_____

_____

_____

_____

MEMORANDUM

TO:
FROM:
DATE:
SUBJECT:

(1) _____
_____
_____

(2) _____
_____
_____

(3)   2005   2004   2003
   Net income (net loss) _____
   Cash flow from operations _____

   Analysis: _____
_____
_____

(4) _____
_____
_____
_____

(5) _____
_____
_____

(6) _____
_____
_____
_____

Teamwork in Action--BTN 16-6
Part 1

(a) _____
_____
_____
_____
_____
_____

(b)   **Similarities**   **Differences**

_____

_____

_____

_____

_____

_____

_____

_____

(c) _____

_____

_____

_____

_____

_____

_____

_____

_____

_____

_____

(d) _____

_____

_____

_____

_____

_____

_____

_____

Part 2

| Adjusting Net Income to Cash Flow from Operating Activities ||
Items to Add	Items to Subtract
a.	
b.	
c.	
d.	

(a)

_____

(b)

_____

(c)

_____

(d)

_____

(1) _____

_____

_____

_____

_____

_____

(2) _____

_____

_____

_____

_____

(3) _____

_____

_____

_____

_____

_____

(1) _____
_____
_____
_____
_____
_____
_____
_____
_____

(2) _____
_____
_____
_____
_____
_____
_____
_____
_____
_____

MEMORANDUM

TO:
FROM:
DATE:
SUBJECT:

(1) _____

_____

(2) _____

_____

_____

_____

_____

_____

(3) _____

_____

_____

_____

_____

Global Decision--BTN 16-11

(1) Cash Flow on Total Assets Ratio _____
    Current Year: _____

_____

    Prior Year: _____

_____

(2) Comparative Analysis: _____

_____

_____

_____

_____
_____
_____
_____
_____

Quick Study 17-2

_____
_____
_____
_____
_____
_____
_____
_____
_____
_____
_____
_____
_____
_____
_____
_____
_____
_____

Quick Study 17-3
(1) Common-Size Percents
    2008 _____
    2007 _____

(2) Trend Percents
    2008 _____
    2007 _____
_____

	2008	2007	Dollar Change	Percent Change

Quick Study 17-5

(1)	(6)
(2)	(7)
(3)	(8)
(4)	(9)
(5)	(10)

Quick Study 17-6

(1)

(2)

(3)

Quick Study 17-7

Ratio	2008	2007	Change
1. Profit Margin Ratio	9%	8%	
2. Debt Ratio	47%	42%	
3. Gross Margin Ratio	34%	46%	
4. Acid-Test Ratio	1.00	1.15	
5. Accounts Receivable Turnover	5.5	6.7	
6. Basic Earnings Per Share	$1.25	$1.10	
7. Inventory Turnover	3.6	3.4	
8. Dividend Yield	2.0%	1.2%	

Quick Study 17-8[A]

	2010	2009	2008	2007	2006

Analysis:

Exercise 17-2

	2008	2007

Analysis:

Exercise 17-4

COMPARATIVE ANALYSIS REPORT

COMPARATIVE ANALYSIS REPORT

Simeon Company Common-Size Comparative Balance Sheets December 31, 2007-2009			
	2009	2008	2007

Analysis and interpretation: _____

_____

_____

_____

_____

_____

_____

_____

_____

_____

(1) Current Ratio:

2009: _____

_____

_____

2008: _____

_____

_____

2007: _____

_____

_____

(2) Acid-test ratio

2009: _____

_____

2008: _____

_____

2007: _____

_____

_____

Analysis and interpretation: _____

_____

_____

_____

_____

_____

_____

1. Days' sales uncollected:

2009: _____

_____

_____

2008: _____

_____

_____

2. Accounts receivable turnover:

2009: _____

_____

_____

2008: _____

_____

_____

3. Inventory turnover:

2009: _____

_____

_____

2008: _____

_____

_____

4. Days' sales in inventory:

2009: _____

_____

2008: _____

_____

_____

Analysis and interpretation:

_____

_____

_____

_____

_____

_____

_____

(1) _____
_____
_____
_____
_____
_____
_____
_____
_____

(2) _____
_____
_____
_____
_____
_____
_____
_____

(3) _____
_____
_____
_____
_____
_____
_____

Analysis and interpretation: _____
_____
_____
_____
_____
_____
_____
_____

(1) Profit margin:

2009: _____

_____

_____

2008: _____

_____

_____

(2) Total asset turnover:

2009: _____

_____

_____

2008: _____

_____

_____

(3) Return on total assets:

2009: _____

_____

_____

2008: _____

_____

_____

Analysis and interpretation: _____

_____

_____

_____

_____

_____

_____

_____

_____

(1) Return on common stockholders' equity:

2009: _____

_____

_____

2008: _____

_____

_____

(2) Price-earnings ratio, December 31:

2009: _____

_____

_____

2008: _____

_____

_____

(3) Dividend yield:

2009: _____

_____

_____

2008: _____

_____

_____

Analysis and interpretation: _____

_____

_____

_____

_____

_____

_____

(1) _____   (5) _____
(2) _____   (6) _____
(3) _____   (7) _____
(4) _____   (8) _____

Exercise 17-13

Randa Merchandising
Income Statement
For Year Ended December 31, 2008

2009: _____
_____
_____

2008: _____
_____
_____

2007: _____
_____
_____

Part 2

Common-Size Comparative Income Statements For Years Ended December 31, 2009, 2008, and 2007	2009	2008	2007

Balance Sheet Data in Trend Percents December 31, 2009, 2008, and 2007	2009	2008	2007

Part 4

Significant relations revealed:

	Income Statement Trends For Years Ended December 31, 2009-2003						
	2009	2008	2007	2006	2005	2004	2003

	Balance Sheet Trends December 31, 2009-2003						
	2009	2008	2007	2006	2005	2004	2003

Analysis and interpretation:

_____

_____

_____

_____

_____

_____

_____

_____

_____

_____

_____

_____

_____

_____

_____

_____

_____

Transaction	Current Assets	Quick Assets	Current Liabilities	Current Ratio	Acid-Test Ratio	Working Capital
Beg. Bal.						

Supporting computations:

(1) Current ratio:

_____

_____

_____

(2) Acid-test ratio:

_____

_____

_____

(3) Days' sales uncollected:

_____

_____

_____

(4) Inventory turnover:

_____

_____

_____

(5) Days' sales in inventory:

_____

_____

_____

(6) Debt-to-equity Ratio:

_____

_____

_____

(7) Times interest earned:

_____

_____

_____

(8) Profit margin ratio:

_____

_____

_____

(9) Total asset turnover:

_____

_____

_____

_____

(10) Return on total assets:

_____

_____

_____

_____

(11) Return on common stockholders' equity:

_____

_____

_____

_____

	Company	Company
a. Current ratio:		
b. Acid-test ratio:		
c. Accounts (incl. notes) receivable turnover:		
d. Inventory turnover:		
e. Days' sales in inventory:		
f. Days' sales uncollected:		
Short-term credit risk analysis:		

	Company	Company
a. Profit margin ratio:		

b. Total asset turnover:

c. Return on total assets:

d. Return on common stockholders' equity:

e. Price-earnings ratio:

f. Dividend yield:

Investment analysis:

Part 1   Effect of Income Taxes:

Items	Pre-Tax	___% Tax Effect	After-Tax

Part 2 Income from Continuing Operations and its Components:

Part 3 Income from Discontinued Segment:

Part 4 Income before Extraordinary Items:

_____

_____

_____

_____

_____

Part 5 Net Income:

_____

_____

_____

_____

_____

_____

(1) Gross Margin Ratio (with services revenue):

_____
_____
_____

Gross Margin Ratio (without services revenue):

_____
_____
_____

Profit Margin Ratio:

_____
_____
_____

(2) Current Ratio:

_____
_____
_____

Acid-Test Ratio:

_____
_____
_____

(3) Debt Ratio:

_____
_____
_____

Equity Ratio:

_____
_____
_____

(4) Current Assets as % of Total Assets:

_____
_____

Long-Term Assets as % of Total Assets:

_____
_____
_____

(1) Trend Percents for selected income statement accounts:

	2005	2004	2003
Revenues			
Cost of Goods Sold			
Selling general and admin. expenses			
Income taxes			
Net income			

(2) Common-size percents for asset categorles and accounts:

	2005	2004
Total current assets		
Property and equipment, net		
Intangible assets		

(3) Analysis and Interpretation:

_____
_____
_____
_____
_____
_____
_____
_____
_____
_____
_____
_____
_____

(4) Fast Forward

_____
_____
_____
_____
_____
_____
_____
_____
_____
_____

(1)

Key figures	Best Buy	Circuit City
Cash and cash equivalents		
Accounts receivable, net		
Inventories		
Retained earnings		
Cost of Goods Sold*		
Revenues		
Total Assets		

* Circuit City's cost of goods sold is titled cost of sales.

(2) _____
_____
_____
_____
_____
_____

(3) _____
_____
_____
_____
_____
_____

(4) _____
_____
_____
_____
_____
_____
_____

(1) _____
_____
_____
_____
_____
_____
_____
_____
_____
_____
_____

(2) _____
_____
_____
_____
_____
_____
_____
_____
_____
_____
_____
_____
_____
_____
_____
_____

MEMORANDUM

TO:

FROM:

DATE:

SUBJECT:

	2004	2003
1. Profit margin ratio		
2. Gross profit ratio		
3. Return on total assets		
4. Return on common stockholders' equity		
5. Basic earnings per share		

Analysis and Interpretation:

Part 1 _____

_____

_____

_____

_____

_____

_____

_____

_____

_____

_____

_____

_____

_____

_____

_____

_____

_____

_____

_____

Part 2 _____

_____

_____

_____

_____

_____

_____

_____

_____

_____

_____

_____

_____

_____

_____

Part 3 _____

_____

(1) _____

_____

(2) _____

_____

(3) _____

_____

(4) _____

_____

_____

Chapter 17   Entrepreneurial Decision   Name _____
          BTN 17-8

(1) _____
_____
_____
_____
_____

(2) _____
_____
_____

(3) _____
_____
_____
_____

(4) _____
_____
_____
_____

(5) _____
_____
_____
_____

(6) _____
_____
_____
_____

Hitting the Road--BTN 17-9

_____
_____
_____
_____
_____
_____
_____
_____

Identification of Differences (more than five exist):

(1) _____

_____

(2) _____

_____

(3) _____

_____

(4) _____

_____

(5) _____

_____

Answer: _____

_____

Quick Study 18-2

(1) _____   (4) _____
(2) _____   (5) _____
(3) _____

Quick Study 18-3

(1) _____   (3) _____
(2) _____   (4) _____

Quick Study 18-4

Answer: _____

_____

Quick Study 18-5

(1) _____   (4) _____
(2) _____   (5) _____
(3) _____

Quick Study 18-6

Answer: _____

_____

Quick Study 18-7

Usual Sequence: _____

_____

_____

Quick Study 18-9

Quick Study 18-10

Briton Company
Manufacturing Statement
For Year Ended December 31, 2008

(a) _____

_____

_____

_____

_____

_____

(b) _____

_____

_____

Quick Study 18-12

_____
_____

_____

_____

_____

_____

_____

_____

_____

_____

Business Decision	Primary Information Source	
	Managerial	Financial
Report financial performance to board of directors		
Estimate product cost for new line of shoes...		
Plan the budget for next quarter................................		
Measure profitability of all individual stores.................		
Prepare financial reports according to GAAP................		
Determine amount of dividends to pay stockholders......		
Determine location and size for a new plant.................		
Evaluate a purchasing department's performance.........		

Exercise 18-2

(1) _____ is the process of setting goals and making plans to achieve them.

(2) _____ is the process of monitoring planning decisions and evaluating the organization's activities and employees.

(3) _____ usually covers a period of 5 to 10 years.

(4) _____ usually covers a period of one year.

	Financial Accounting	Managerial Accounting
1. Users and decision makers		
2. Purpose of information		
3. Flexibility of practice		
4. Timeliness of information		
5. Time dimension		
6. Focus of information		
7. Nature of information		

(a) _____

| (1) _____ | (3) _____ |
| (2) _____ | (4) _____ |

(b) _____
_____
_____
_____
_____
_____

Exercise 18-5

(1) _____
(2) _____
(3) _____

Exercise 18-6

	Product Cost		Period Cost	Direct Cost	Indirect Cost
	Prime	Conversion			
Direct materials used...............					
State and federal income taxes					
Payroll taxes for production supervisor.............................					
Amortization of patents on factory machine.......................					
Accident insurance on factory workers...............................					
Wages to assembly workers.......					
Factory utilities........................					
Small tools used.......................					
Bad debts expense...................					
Depreciation--Factory building....					
Advertising.............................					
Office supplies used.................					

(1) Cost classifications:

(a) _____   (d) _____

(b) _____   (e) _____

(c) _____

(2) Purpose:

_____

_____

_____

_____

_____

_____

_____

_____

_____

_____

_____

(1)

Product Costs	Cost by Behavior		Cost by Traceability	
	Variable	Fixed	Direct	Indirect
Annual flat fee paid for office security............................				
Leather cover for soccer balls...........				
Lace to hold the leather together......				
Wages of assembly workers.............				
Taxes on factory............................				
Coolants for machinery...................				
Machinery depreciation...................				

(2) _____

_____

_____

_____

_____

_____

_____

_____

_____

_____

(1) Identification: _____

_____
_____
_____
_____

(2)

| Company 1 |
| Sun Fresh Foods |
| Current Asset Section |
| December 31, 2008 |

_____
_____
_____
_____
_____
_____
_____
_____
_____
_____

| Company 2 |
| Salomon Skis Mfg. |
| Current Asset Section |
| December 31, 2008 |

_____
_____
_____
_____
_____
_____
_____
_____
_____
_____

Discussion: _____

_____
_____
_____
_____

Merchandising Business

Viking Retail
Partial Income Statement
For Year Ended December 31, 2008

Manufacturing Business

Log Homes Manufacturing
Partial Income Statement
For Year Ended December 31, 2008

	Garcia Company	Culpepper Company
(1) COST OF GOODS MANUFACTURED		

(2) COST OF GOODS SOLD

Name _____

Account	Balance Sheet	Income Statement	Manufacturing Statement	Overhead Report
Accounts receivable.............				
Computer supplies used in office................................				
Beginning finished goods inventory............................				
Beginning goods in process inventory............................				
Beginning raw materials inventory............................				
Cash................................				
Depreciation expense-Factory building............................				
Depreciation expense-Factory equipment..........................				
Depreciation expense-Office building............................				
Depreciation expense-Office equipment..........................				
Direct labor.........................				
Ending finished goods inventory............................				
Ending goods in process inventory............................				
Ending raw materials inventory............................				
Factory maintenance wages..				
Computer supplies used in factory.............................				
Income taxes.....................				
Insurance on factory building				
Rent cost on office building...				
Office supplies used..............				
Property taxes on factory building............................				
Raw materials purchases........				
Sales................................				

Name _____

Shanta Company
Manufacturing Statement
For Year Ended December 31, 2008

Shanta Company
Income Statement
For Year Ended December 31, 2008

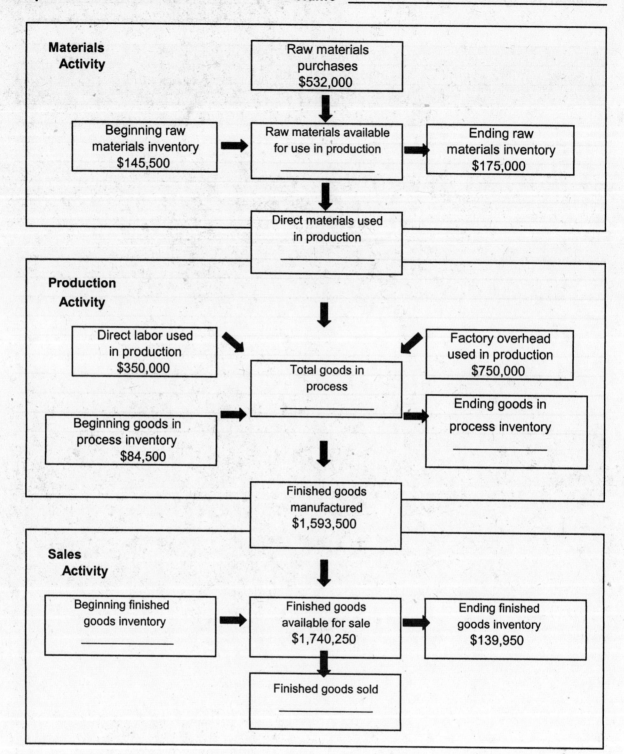

Materials Activity

Raw materials purchases $532,000

Beginning raw materials inventory $145,500

Raw materials available for use in production _____

Ending raw materials inventory $175,000

Direct materials used in production _____

Production Activity

Direct labor used in production $350,000

Factory overhead used in production $750,000

Total goods in process _____

Beginning goods in process inventory $84,500

Ending goods in process inventory _____

Finished goods manufactured $1,593,500

Sales Activity

Beginning finished goods inventory _____

Finished goods available for sale $1,740,250

Ending finished goods inventory $139,950

Finished goods sold _____

Managerial accounting contributions and responsibilities:

_____
_____
_____
_____
_____
_____
_____
_____
_____
_____
_____
_____
_____
_____
_____

Problem 18-2A or 18-2B

(1) _____	(6) _____
(2) _____	(7) _____
(3) _____	(8) _____
(4) _____	(9) _____
(5) _____	(10) _____

Part 1

Costs	Cost by Behavior		Cost by Function	
	Variable	Fixed	Product	Period

Part 2

Computation of Manufacturing Cost per _____ For Year Ended December 31, 2008	Total Cost	Per Unit Cost
Variable costs		
Fixed Costs		

Part 3

_____

_____

_____

_____

_____

Part 4

_____

_____

_____

MEMORANDUM

TO:

FROM:

DATE:

SUBJECT: Cost classification and explanation

Cost Estimation (including opportunity costs): _____

Units and Dollar Amounts for Raw Materials Inventory

_____
_____
_____
_____
_____
_____
_____
_____
_____

Part 2

MEMORANDUM

TO:
FROM:
DATE:
SUBJECT: Consideration of JIT inventory system

_____
_____
_____
_____
_____
_____
_____
_____
_____
_____
_____
_____
_____
_____
_____
_____
_____

Merchandising Business

_____

Partial Income Statement
For Year Ended December 31, 2008

Manufacturing Business

_____

Partial Income Statement
For Year Ended December 31, 2008

MEMORANDUM

TO:

FROM:

DATE:

SUBJECT: Identifying and reporting inventory accounts

Manufacturing Statement
For Year Ended December 31, 2008

Income Statement
For Year Ended December 31, 2008

Inventory Ratios	Raw Materials	Finished Goods

Analysis and discussion:

_____
_____
_____
_____
_____
_____
_____
_____
_____
_____
_____
_____
_____

Name _____

Part 1
_____
_____
_____
_____
_____
_____
_____
_____

Part 2
_____
_____
_____
_____
_____
_____
_____
_____
_____

Part 3
_____
_____
_____
_____
_____
_____
_____
_____
_____
_____
_____

(1)

Product Costs	Cost by Behavior		Cost by Traceability	
	Variable	Fixed	Direct	Indirect
Glue to assemble workstation component parts......................				
Laminate coverings for desktops....				
Wages of desk assembler..............				
Taxes on assembly workshop........				
Depreciation on tools...................				
Electricity for workshop.................				
Monthly flat fee to clean workshop.				

(2)

Success Systems
Manufacturing Statement
For Month Ended January 31, 2009

(3)

Success Systems
Partial Income Statement
For Month Ended January 31, 2009

Cost of goods sold

(1)

Estimate	Effects if Actual Results differ from Assumptions

(2)

(3) Fast Forward:

(1)

Best Buy

_____

_____

_____

_____

_____

_____

Circuit City

_____

_____

_____

_____

_____

_____

(2)

_____

_____

_____

_____

_____

_____

_____

(1) Account Identification

_____
_____
_____
_____
_____
_____
_____
_____

(2) CFO Response

_____
_____
_____
_____
_____
_____
_____
_____
_____
_____
_____
_____

MEMORANDUM

TO:
FROM:
DATE:
SUBJECT: Business student salary expectations

Summary of Ethical Standards: _____

_____

_____

_____

_____

_____

_____

_____

_____

_____

_____

_____

_____

Attach printout of IMA Ethical Standards

_____

_____

_____

_____

_____

_____

_____

_____

_____

_____

_____

_____

_____

_____

_____

_____

_____

_____

_____

_____

_____

_____

_____

_____

_____

_____

_____

_____

_____

_____

_____

_____

_____

_____

_____

_____

_____

_____

_____

_____

_____

_____

_____

_____

_____

_____

(1) _____

_____

_____

_____

_____

_____

_____

_____

_____

(2) _____

_____

_____

_____

_____

_____

_____

_____

_____

(1) Manufacturing Cost Categories _____

_____

_____

_____

_____

_____

_____

_____

(2) Managerial Measures _____

_____

_____

_____

_____

_____

_____

_____

_____

(1) Customer Business Activities (from arrival through departure)

_____
_____
_____
_____
_____

(2) Costs of Customer Business Activities from Part 1

_____
_____
_____
_____
_____
_____
_____

(3) Cost Classification and Explanation

_____
_____
_____
_____
_____
_____
_____

(1) Responsibilities _____

_____

_____

_____

_____

_____

_____

_____

_____

_____

_____

(2) Involvement _____

_____

_____

_____

_____

_____

_____

_____

_____

_____

_____

_____

_____

Name _____

(1) Overhead as Percent of Direct Labor

_____

_____

(2) Overhead as Percent of Direct Materials

_____

_____

Quick Study 19-2

Job: _____

Job lot: _____

Quick Study 19-3

Job Cost Sheet

_____
_____
_____
_____
_____
_____
_____
_____
_____
_____

GENERAL JOURNAL

Date		Account Titles and Explanation	P. R.	Debit	Credit

Quick Study 19-5

GENERAL JOURNAL

Date		Account Titles and Explanation	P. R.	Debit	Credit

Quick Study 19-6

GENERAL JOURNAL

Date		Account Titles and Explanation	P. R.	Debit	Credit

Name _____

GENERAL JOURNAL

Date	Account Titles and Explanation	P. R.	Debit	Credit

Computations: _____

_____

_____

_____

_____

(1) _____   (5) _____
(2) _____   (6) _____
(3) _____   (7) _____
(4) _____

Exercise 19-2

(1) _____

_____

_____

_____

_____

_____

_____

_____

(2) _____

_____

_____

_____

_____

_____

_____

_____

(3) _____

_____

_____

_____

_____

_____

_____

_____

(4) _____

_____

_____

_____

_____

_____

_____

Exercise 19-3

(1) Predetermined Overhead Rate _____

_____

_____

(2) _____

_____

_____

_____

_____

Exercise 19-4

(1) Predetermined Overhead Rate _____

_____

_____

(2) _____

_____

_____

_____

_____

Name _____

(1) Cost of Direct Materials Used

_____

_____

_____

_____

_____

_____

_____

_____

(2) Cost of Direct Labor Used

_____

_____

_____

_____

_____

(3) Cost of Goods Manufactured

_____

_____

_____

_____

_____

_____

_____

_____

_____

(4) Cost of Goods Sold

_____

_____

_____

_____

_____

_____

_____

(5) Gross Profit

_____
_____
_____
_____
_____
_____

(6) Overapplied or Underapplied Overhead

_____
_____
_____
_____
_____
_____
_____

Name _____

GENERAL JOURNAL

Date	Account Titles and Explanation	P. R.	Debit	Credit
(1)				
(2)				
(3)				
(4)				
(5)				
(6)				
(7)				

Name _____

GENERAL JOURNAL

Date	Account Titles and Explanation	P. R.	Debit	Credit
(8)				
(9)				
(10)				
(11)				

Exercise 19-7

(1) Predetermined Overhead Rate _____

_____

_____

_____

_____

_____

(2 & 3) _____

_____

_____

_____

_____

_____

_____

_____

_____

(4)

GENERAL JOURNAL

Date		Account Titles and Explanation	P. R.	Debit	Credit

Exercise 19-8

(1) Predetermined Overhead Rate _____

_____

_____

_____

_____

_____

(2 & 3) _____

_____

_____

_____

_____

_____

_____

_____

_____

_____

_____

(4)

GENERAL JOURNAL

Date	Account Titles and Explanation	P. R.	Debit	Credit

(5)

GENERAL JOURNAL

Date	Account Titles and Explanation	P. R.	Debit	Credit

Supporting Computations

_____

_____

_____

_____

_____

(1) Predetermined Overhead Rate _____

_____

_____

_____

(2) Direct Materials Costs

_____

_____

_____

_____

_____

(3) Direct Labor Costs and Overhead Costs _____

_____

_____

_____

_____

_____

_____

_____

_____

_____

Exercise 19-10

(1) Predetermined Overhead Rate _____

_____

_____

_____

_____

(2)

	Goods in Process			Finished Goods		
	Cost per Unit	Units	Total Cost	Cost per Unit	Units	Total Cost
Direct materials						
Direct labor						
Overhead						
Total						

(3) _____

_____

_____

_____

_____

_____

_____

_____

_____

_____

_____

_____

_____

_____

_____

_____

_____

_____

_____

_____

Name _____

(1) Estimated Cost of the Architectural Job

(2) Suggested Bid Price

Total Manufacturing Costs and Costs Assigned to Each Job

Costs	Job_____	Job_____	Job_____	Total for Month

GENERAL JOURNAL

Date	Account Titles and Explanation	P. R.	Debit	Credit
(a)				
(b)				

GENERAL JOURNAL

Date		Account Titles and Explanation	P. R.	Debit	Credit
(c)					
(d)					
(e)					
(f)					

	Manufacturing Statement	
	For Month Ended _____	

Gross Profit Computation

_____
_____
_____
_____
_____
_____
_____

Presentation of Inventories on Balance Sheet

_____
_____
_____
_____
_____
_____
_____
_____
_____

Part 5

Impacts of Over- or Underapplied Overhead

_____
_____
_____
_____
_____

GENERAL JOURNAL

Date	Account Titles and Explanation	P. R.	Debit	Credit
(a)				
(b)				
(c)				
(d)				
(e)				

GENERAL JOURNAL

Date	Account Titles and Explanation	P. R.	Debit	Credit

Overhead computations:

_____
_____
_____
_____
_____
_____
_____
_____
_____

Part 3

Trial Balance
December 31, 2008

	Debit	Credit

_____
_____
_____
_____
_____
_____
_____
_____
_____
_____
_____
_____
_____
_____
_____
_____
_____
_____
_____

Income Statement
For Year Ended December 31, 2008

_____
_____
_____
_____
_____
_____
_____
_____

Balance Sheet
December 31, 2008

_____
_____
_____
_____
_____
_____
_____
_____
_____
_____
_____
_____
_____
_____
_____
_____
_____

Part 5

Error Analysis for Financial Statements _____

_____
_____
_____
_____
_____
_____

JOB COST SHEETS

```
Job No. _____
Materials...........  _____
Labor...............  _____
Overhead.........  _____
Total Cost.........
```

```
Job No. _____
Materials.........  _____
Labor...............  _____
Overhead.........  _____
Total Cost.........
```

```
Job No. _____
Materials.........  _____
Labor...............  _____
Overhead.........  _____
Total Cost.........
```

```
Job No. _____
Materials.........  _____
Labor...............  _____
Overhead.........  _____
Total Cost.........
```

```
Job No. _____
Materials.........  _____
Labor..............  _____
Overhead.........  _____
Total Cost.........
```

GENERAL JOURNAL

Date	Account Titles and Explanation	P. R.	Debit	Credit
(a)				
(b)				
(c)				
(d)				
(e)				
(f)				
(g)				

GENERAL JOURNAL

Date	Account Titles and Explanation	P. R.	Debit	Credit
(h)				
(i)				
(j)				

Part 3

GENERAL LEDGER ACCOUNTS

Raw Materials Inventory

Factory Payroll

Goods in Process Inventory

Factory Overhead

Finished Goods Inventory

Cost of Goods Sold

Reports of Job Costs

Goods in Process Inventory:

_____
_____
_____
_____

Finished Goods Inventory:

_____
_____
_____
_____

Cost of Goods Sold:

_____
_____
_____
_____

Problem 19-4A or 19-4B
Part 1

(a) Predetermined Overhead Rate _____

_____
_____
_____
_____
_____

(b) Overhead Costs Applied to Jobs

Job No.	Direct Labor	Applied Overhead
_____		
_____		
_____		
_____		
_____		
Totals..................		

(c) Overapplied or Underapplied Overhead

_____

_____

_____

_____

_____

_____

Part 2

GENERAL JOURNAL

Date		Account Titles and Explanation	P. R.	Debit	Credit

JOB COST SHEET

Customer's Name _____ **Company** _____ **Job No.** _____

	Direct Materials			Direct Labor			Overhead Costs Applied	
Date	Requisition Number	Amount	Date	Time Ticket Number	Amount	Date	Rate	Amount
						SUMMARY OF COSTS		
						Dir. Materials..		_____
						Dir. Labor......		_____
						Overhead......		_____
Total			Total			Total Cost of		
						the Job.........		_____

JOB COST SHEET

Customer's Name _____ **Company** _____ **Job No.** _____

	Direct Materials			Direct Labor			Overhead Costs Applied	
Date	Requisition Number	Amount	Date	Time Ticket Number	Amount	Date	Rate	Amount
						SUMMARY OF COSTS		
						Dir. Materials..		_____
						Dir. Labor......		_____
						Overhead......		_____
Total			Total			Total Cost of		
						the Job.........		_____

MATERIALS LEDGER CARD

Item _____

	Received				Issued				Balance		
Date	Receiving Report	Units	Unit Price	Total Price	Requi-sition	Units	Unit Price	Total Price	Units	Unit Price	Total Price

MATERIALS LEDGER CARD

Item _____

	Received				Issued				Balance		
Date	Receiving Report	Units	Unit Price	Total Price	Requi-sition	Units	Unit Price	Total Price	Units	Unit Price	Total Price

MATERIALS LEDGER CARD

Item _____

	Received				Issued				Balance		
Date	Receiving Report	Units	Unit Price	Total Price	Requi-sition	Units	Unit Price	Total Price	Units	Unit Price	Total Price

GENERAL JOURNAL

Date	Account Titles and Explanation	P. R.	Debit	Credit

GENERAL LEDGER

Cash	Accounts Receivable

Sales	Cost of Goods Sold

Finished Goods Inventory	Accounts Payable

Raw Materials Inventory	Goods in Process Inventory

Factory Overhead	Factory Payroll

FACTORY OVERHEAD LEDGER

Indirect Materials	Indirect Labor

Miscellaneous Overhead	

(1) Cost of Direct Materials Used in Period for each Job and its Total

_____
_____
_____
_____
_____
_____
_____

(2) Cost of Direct Labor Incurred in Period

_____
_____
_____
_____
_____
_____
_____
_____
_____
_____

(3) Predetermined Overhead Rate for Period

_____
_____
_____
_____
_____
_____
_____
_____
_____

(4) Cost Transferred to Finished Goods Inventory in Period

_____
_____
_____
_____
_____
_____
_____
_____

(1) Costs that will Predictably Increase as a Percent of Sales
_____
_____
_____
_____
_____
_____
_____
_____
_____

(2) Explanation and Performance Assessment of the Costs in Part 1
_____
_____
_____
_____
_____
_____
_____
_____
_____
_____
_____
_____

(3) Fast Forward:
_____
_____
_____
_____
_____
_____
_____
_____
_____
_____
_____
_____
_____

Best Buy	Current Year	One Year Prior	Two Years Prior
Inventory change...........			
Operating cash flow effect from inventory change....			

Circuit City	Current Year	One Year Prior	Two Years Prior
Inventory change...........			
Operating cash flow effect from inventory change....			

Part 2

Impacts of JIT Inventory System

_____
_____
_____
_____
_____
_____
_____
_____
_____

Part 3

Operating Cash Flow Impacts of JIT Inventory System

_____
_____
_____
_____
_____
_____
_____
_____

MEMORANDUM

TO:

FROM:

DATE:

SUBJECT: Review of Overhead Allocations

(1) Cost Accounting System Recommendation and Explanation

_____
_____
_____
_____
_____
_____
_____
_____
_____
_____
_____
_____
_____

(2) Document Description for Proposed Cost Accounting System

_____
_____
_____
_____
_____
_____
_____
_____
_____
_____
_____
_____
_____

(3) Document Facilitation of Cost Accounting System

_____
_____
_____
_____
_____
_____
_____
_____
_____
_____
_____
_____

MEMORANDUM

TO:

FROM:

DATE:

SUBJECT: Explanation and recommendation of job order costing software

(1) Appropriateness of Job Order Cost Accounting System

_____
_____
_____
_____
_____
_____
_____
_____
_____
_____
_____

(2) Factors Indicative of Job Order System

_____
_____
_____
_____
_____
_____
_____
_____
_____
_____
_____

Cost Structure Rationale _____

_____

_____

_____

_____

_____

_____

_____

_____

_____

_____

_____

_____

_____

_____

(1) _____

_____

_____

_____

_____

_____

_____

_____

(2) _____

_____

_____

_____

_____

_____

_____

_____

_____

_____

_____

(1)

JOB COST SHEET

Customer's Name _____ Company _____ Job No. _____

	Direct Materials			Direct Labor			Overhead Costs Applied	
Date	Requisition Number	Amount	Date	Time Ticket Number	Amount	Date	Rate	Amount
						SUMMARY OF COSTS		
						Dir. Materials _____		
						Dir. Labor..... _____		
						Overhead.....		
Total			Total			Total Cost of		
						the Job........ _____		

Explanation for Overhead Applied: _____

_____

_____

_____

(2) Report Actual Job Cost Sheet and Compare to Your Own in Part 1

(1) Dixons | **Current Year** | **One Year Prior**

Inventory change...

Operating cash flow effect from inventory change..

(2) Implications of JIT Inventory Systems

_____

_____

_____

_____

_____

_____

_____

_____

Best Buy | **Current Year** | **One Year Prior** | **Two Years Prior**

Inventory change............

Operating cash flow effect from inventory change..

Circuit City | **Current Year** | **One Year Prior** | **Two Years Prior**

Inventory change............

Operating cash flow effect from inventory change..

(1) _____   (6) _____

(2) _____   (7) _____

(3) _____   (8) _____

(4) _____   (9) _____

(5) _____   (10) _____

Quick Study 20-2

GENERAL JOURNAL

Date		Account Titles and Explanation	P. R.	Debit	Credit

Quick Study 20-3

GENERAL JOURNAL

Date		Account Titles and Explanation	P. R.	Debit	Credit

GENERAL JOURNAL

Date		Account Titles and Explanation	P. R.	Debit	Credit

Quick Study 20-5

GENERAL JOURNAL

Date		Account Titles and Explanation	P. R.	Debit	Credit

Quick Study 20-6

EUP for Labor	Equivalent Units

The cost of beginning inventory plus the costs added during the period should equal the cost of units_____plus the cost of _____.

Quick Study 20-8

Explanation of Hybrid Costing System _____
_____
_____

Product or Service Identification for Hybrid Costing System _____
_____
_____
_____

Quick Study 20-9[A]

EUP for Labor	Equivalent Units

(1) _____   (5) _____
(2) _____   (6) _____
(3) _____   (7) _____
(4) _____

Exercise 20-2

GENERAL JOURNAL

Date		Account Titles and Explanation	P. R.	Debit	Credit
1.					
2.					
3.					
4.					
5.					
6.					

GENERAL JOURNAL

Date	Account Titles and Explanation	P. R.	Debit	Credit
7.				
8.				
9.				
10.				

(a) _____

(b) _____

(c) _____

(d) _____

(e) _____

(f) _____

(g) _____

(h) _____

(i) _____

(j) _____

_____

GENERAL JOURNAL

Date	Account Titles and Explanation	P. R.	Debit	Credit
1.				
2.				
3.				
4.				
5.				

Name _____

(1) Units Transferred to Finished Goods _____

_____

_____

_____

_____

_____

(2)

Equivalent units of production	Direct Materials	Direct Labor

1.

Cost per equivalent unit	Direct Materials	Direct Labor

2. Cost Assignment and Reconciliation

Name _____

Equivalent units of production	Direct Materials	Direct Labor

Exercise 20-8^A

1. Cost per equivalent unit of direct materials and direct labor

	Direct Materials	Direct Labor

2. Assignment of costs to output of department

	Direct Materials	Direct Labor

Exercise 20-9

(1)

EUP for Materials

(2)

EUP for Materials

Name _____

(3)

EUP for Materials

_____
_____
_____
_____
_____

Exercise 20-10[A]

(1)

EUP for Materials

_____
_____
_____
_____
_____

(2)

EUP for Materials

_____
_____
_____
_____
_____

(3)

EUP for Materials

_____
_____
_____
_____
_____

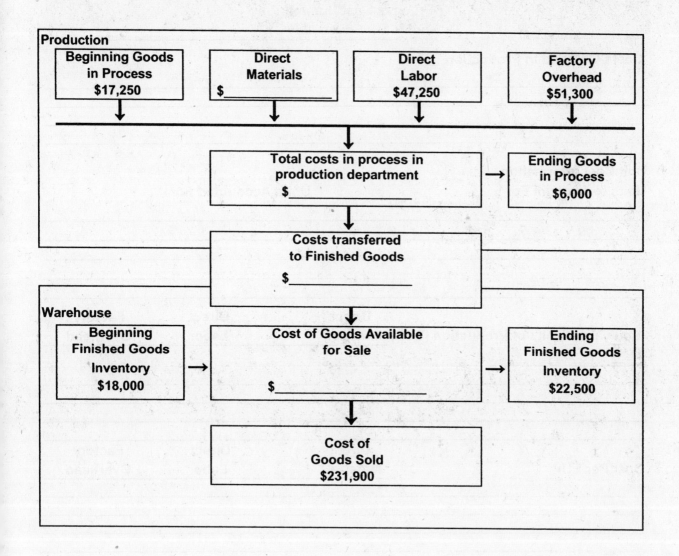

ASHAD COMPANY
Process Cost Summary
For Month Ended July 31

Costs Charged to Production

_____
_____
_____
_____

Unit Cost Information

Units to Account For	Units Accounted For

_____
_____
_____
_____

Equivalent Units of Production (EUP)	Direct Materials	Direct Labor	Factory Overhead

Cost Per EUP	Direct Materials	Direct Labor	Factory Overhead

Cost Assignment and Reconciliation

_____
_____
_____
_____
_____
_____
_____
_____
_____
_____
_____

HI-TEST COMPANY
Process Cost Summary
For Month Ended September 30

Costs Charged to Production

Costs of Beginning work in process

Direct materials...	$45,000	
Direct Labor..	25,600	
Factory Overhead..	30,720	$101,320
Costs incurred this period..		
Direct materials..	375,000	
Direct Labor..	155,000	
Factory Overhead ($155,000 x 120%)	(a) _____	(b) _____
Total costs to account for...		(c) _____

Unit Cost Information

Units to Account For		Units Accounted For	
Beginning goods in process...	2,000	Completed & transferred out.......	23,000
Units started this period........	28,000	Ending goods in process.............	(d) _____
Total units to account for..... (e) _____		Total units accounted for............	(f) _____

Equivalent Units of Production (EUP)	Direct Materials	Direct Labor	Factory Overhead
Units completed and transferred out...	(g)_____EUP	(h)_____EUP	(I)_____EUP
Units of ending goods in process			
Direct materials [(j)_____ x 100%]......	(k)_____EUP		
Direct labor [(l)_____ x 40%].............		(m)_____EUP	
Factory overhead [(n)_____ x 40%]....			(o)_____EUP
Equivalent units of production...........	(p)_____EUP	(q)_____EUP	(r)_____EUP

Cost per EUP	Direct Materials	Direct Labor	Factory Overhead
Costs of beginning goods in process...	$ 45,000	$ 25,600	$30,720
Costs incurred this period...................	375,000	155,000	(s) _____
Total costs...	$420,000	$180,600	(t) $_____
÷ Equivalent units of production...........	(u)_____	(v)_____	(w)_____
Cost per equivalent unit of production..	(x) $_____/EUP	(y) $____/EUP	(z) $_____/EUP

(continued on next page)

Cost Assignment and Reconciliation
Costs transferred out
   Direct materials [(aa)$_____ x (bb)_____]..................... (cc) $_____
   Direct labor [(dd)$_____ x (ee)_____]........................... (ff)   _____
   Factory overhead [(gg)$_____ x (hh)_____].................. (ii)   _____
   Total transferred out... (jj) $_____
Cost of ending good in process
   Direct materials [(kk)$_____ x (ll)_____]...................... (mm) _____
   Direct labor [(nn)$_____ x (oo)_____].............................. (pp)   _____
   Factory overhead [(qq)$_____ x (rr)_____].................... (ss)   _____
   Total ending goods in process.. (tt) _____
Total costs accounted for.. (uu) $_____

Cost of goods transferred and cost of goods sold

_____

_____
_____
_____
_____
_____
_____
_____
_____
_____
_____
_____
_____
_____
_____

Part 2

GENERAL JOURNAL

Date	Account Titles and Explanation	P. R.	Debit	Credit
a.				
b.				
c.				
d.				

GENERAL JOURNAL

Date	Account Titles and Explanation	P. R.	Debit	Credit
e.				
f.				
g.				
h.				
i.				
j.				

(a and b)

Equivalent units of production	Direct Materials	Direct Labor

Part 2

Costs per equivalent unit	Direct Materials	Direct Labor

Assignment of product costs to units

_____
_____
_____
_____
_____
_____
_____
_____
_____
_____
_____

MEMORANDUM

TO:

FROM:

DATE:

SUBJECT: Percentage of completion error analysis

GENERAL JOURNAL

Date		Account Titles and Explanation	P. R.	Debit	Credit
a.					
b.					
c.					
d.					
e.					
f.					
g.					
h.					
i.					
j.					

Process Cost Summary

For Month Ended _____

Costs Charged to Production

_____

_____

_____

_____

_____

_____

_____

_____

Unit Cost Information

Units to Account For   **Units Accounted For**

_____

_____

_____

_____

Equivalent Units of Production (EUP)	**Direct Materials**	**Direct Labor**	**Factory Overhead**

Cost per EUP	**Direct Materials**	**Direct Labor**	**Factory Overhead**

Cost Assignment and Reconciliation

_____

_____

_____

_____

_____

_____

_____

_____

_____

_____

_____

_____

_____

_____
_____
_____
_____
_____
_____
_____
_____
_____
_____

Process Cost Summary
For Month Ended _____

Costs Charged to Production

_____
_____
_____
_____
_____
_____
_____
_____
_____
_____

Unit Cost Information

Units to Account For	Units Accounted For

Equivalent Units of Production (EUP)	Direct Materials	Direct Labor	Factory Overhead

Cost per EUP	Direct Materials	Direct Labor	Factory Overhead

Cost Assignment and Reconciliation

_____
_____
_____
_____
_____
_____
_____
_____
_____
_____
_____
_____

GENERAL JOURNAL

Date		Account Titles and Explanation	P. R.	Debit	Credit

Name _____

Process Cost Summary
For Month Ended _____

Costs Charged to Production

_____
_____
_____
_____
_____
_____
_____
_____
_____
_____

Unit Cost Information
Units to Account For   **Units Accounted For**

_____
_____
_____
_____

Equivalent Units of Production (EUP)	**Direct Materials**	**Direct Labor**	**Factory Overhead**

Cost per EUP	**Direct Materials**	**Direct Labor**	**Factory Overhead**

Process cost summary continued on next page.

Cost Assignment and Reconciliation

_____
_____
_____
_____
_____
_____
_____
_____
_____
_____
_____

Part 2

GENERAL JOURNAL

Date		Account Titles and Explanation	P. R.	Debit	Credit

Part 3

(a)
_____
_____
_____

(b)
_____
_____
_____
_____
_____
_____

Process Cost Summary
For Month Ended _____

Costs Charged to Production

_____

_____

_____

_____

_____

_____

_____

_____

_____

_____

Unit Cost Information
Units to Account For   **Units Accounted For**

_____

_____

_____

_____

Equivalent Units of Production (EUP)	**Direct Materials**	**Direct Labor**	**Factory Overhead**

Cost per EUP	**Direct Materials**	**Direct Labor**	**Factory Overhead**

┌───┐
│   Process cost summary continued on next page.   │
└───┘

Cost Assignment and Reconciliation

_____
_____
_____
_____
_____
_____
_____
_____
_____
_____
_____
_____
_____
_____
_____
_____

Part 2

GENERAL JOURNAL

Date		Account Titles and Explanation	P. R.	Debit	Credit

Job Order Costing	Process Cosing

Part 2

_____

_____

_____

_____

_____

_____

[Note: General Ledger accounts shown in Part 4.]

GENERAL JOURNAL

Date		Account Titles and Explanation	P. R.	Debit	Credit
(a)					
(b)					
(c)					
(d)					
(e)					
(f)					

Process Cost Summary
For Month Ended _____

Costs Charged to Production

_____

_____

_____

_____

_____

_____

_____

_____

_____

_____

Unit Cost Information
Units to Account For   **Units Accounted For**

_____

_____

_____

_____

Equivalent Units of Production (EUP)	Direct Materials	Direct Labor	Factory Overhead

Cost per EUP	Direct Materials	Direct Labor	Factory Overhead

Process cost summary continued on next page.

_____
_____
_____
_____
_____
_____
_____
_____
_____
_____
_____

Part 3

GENERAL JOURNAL

Date	Account Titles and Explanation	P. R.	Debit	Credit
(g)				
(h)				

General Ledger accounts:

		Raw Materials Inventory			ACCOUNT NO. 132	
Date	Explanation	P.R.	DEBIT	CREDIT	BALANCE
June 30	Balance				50,000

		Goods in Process Inventory			ACCOUNT NO. 133	
Date	Explanation	P.R.	DEBIT	CREDIT	BALANCE
June 30	Balance				16,270

Finished Goods Inventory   ACCOUNT NO. 135

Date	Explanation	P.R.	DEBIT	CREDIT	BALANCE
June 30	Balance				220,000

Sales   ACCOUNT NO. 413

Date	Explanation	P.R.	DEBIT	CREDIT	BALANCE

Cost of Goods Sold   ACCOUNT NO. 502

Date	Explanation	P.R.	DEBIT	CREDIT	BALANCE

Factory Payroll   ACCOUNT NO. 530

Date	Explanation	P.R.	DEBIT	CREDIT	BALANCE

Factory Overhead   ACCOUNT NO. 540

Date	Explanation	P.R.	DEBIT	CREDIT	BALANCE

Part 5
Computation of gross profit for July:

_____

_____

_____

_____

_____

_____
_____
_____
_____
_____
_____
_____
_____

Part 2

_____
_____
_____
_____
_____
_____
_____

Part 3 - Fast Forward:

_____
_____
_____
_____
_____
_____
_____
_____
_____
_____

	Best Buy		Circuit City	
	Current Year	Prior Year	Current Year	Prior Year
COGS/ Total expenses				

Part 2

Analysis and Comparison of Cost Structures: _____

_____

_____

_____

_____

_____

_____

_____

MEMORANDUM

TO:

FROM:

DATE:

SUBJECT: Action plan to understand business processes

_____

_____

_____

_____

_____

_____

_____

_____

_____

_____

_____

_____

_____

_____

_____

_____

_____

_____

_____

_____

_____

_____

_____

_____

_____

_____

_____

_____

_____

_____

_____

_____

_____

_____

_____

_____

_____

_____

_____

MEMORANDUM

TO:

FROM:

DATE:

SUBJECT: Explanation of cost classifications

_____
_____
_____
_____
_____
_____
_____
_____
_____
_____
_____
_____
_____

GENERAL JOURNAL

Date	Account Titles and Explanation	P. R.	Debit	Credit

(1) _____
_____
_____
_____
_____
_____

(2) _____
_____
_____
_____
_____
_____

(3) _____
_____
_____
_____
_____
_____

Entrepreneurial Decision BTN 20-8

_____
_____
_____
_____
_____
_____
_____
_____
_____
_____
_____
_____
_____

Cost description	Direct Materials	Direct Labor	Overhead	Variable cost	Fixed cost

Overhead allocation suggestions:

1. **Ratio of Cost of Goods Sold to Total Expenses**

	Current Year	Prior Year
Dixons............		

	Current Year	Prior Year
Best Buy................		

	Current Year	Prior Year
Circuit City.......................		

2. **Similarities or Differences Across Years and Companies:** _____
_____
_____
_____
_____
_____
_____
_____

(1) _____   (5) _____
(2) _____   (6) _____
(3) _____   (7) _____
(4) _____

Quick Study 21-2

(1) _____

_____

(2) _____

_____

(3) _____

_____

(4) _____

_____

_____

Quick Study 21-3

Total Overhead Allocated to Operating Department 1: _____

_____
_____
_____
_____
_____
_____
_____
_____
_____
_____
_____
_____

Contribution to Overhead (dollars):

Dept. A	
Dept. B	
Dept. C	

Contribution to Overhead (percent of sales):

Dept. A	
Dept. B	
Dept. C	

Highest Contribution (Dollar & Percent)

_____

_____

_____

Quick Study 21-5

Center	Net Income	Average Assets	Return on Assets
Basketball	$ 4,500,000	$ 20,000,000	
Soccer	1,500,000	12,500,000	
Cross-trainer	800,000	10,000,000	

Center Performance Evaluation:

_____

_____

_____

_____

Quick Study 21-6[A]

Joint Cost Assigned to Unit B Using the Value Basis of Allocation

_____

_____

_____

_____

_____

_____

_____

_____

_____

_____

_____

_____

(1) Allocation of Indirect Expenses to Operating Departments

Supervision:

	Employees	% of Total	Cost
Materials			
Personnel			
Manufacturing			
Packaging			
Totals			

Utilities:

	Square Feet	% of Total	Cost
Materials			
Personnel			
Manufacturing			
Packaging			
Totals			

Insurance:

	Assets Value	% of Total	Cost
Materials			
Personnel			
Manufacturing			
Packaging			
Totals			

(2) Total indirect expenses assigned to operating departments:

	Supervision	Utilities	Insurance	Totals
Materials				
Personnel				
Manufacturing				
Packaging				
Totals				

Preliminary Computations (predetermined overhead rates)

Overhead Cost Pool	Total Cost	Amount of Cost Driver	Predetermined Overhead Rate
Supervision			
Depreciation			
Line Preparation			

(1) Assignment of overhead costs to the two products using ABC

Rounded edge:

	Cost Driver	Cost per Driver Unit	Allocated Cost
Supervision			
Machinery depreciation			
Line preparation			
Total overhead assigned			

Squared edge:

	Cost Driver	Cost per Driver Unit	Allocated Cost
Supervision			
Machinery depreciation			
Line preparation			
Total overhead assigned			

(3) Comparison of Cost Allocation Methods

_____

_____

_____

_____

_____

_____

Step 1: Allocate total rent expense among the floors.

Exercise 21-3

	Amount Allocated	% of Total	Cost
First floor			
Second floor			
Totals			

Step 2: Allocate the floors' rent expense to the separate departments.

First Floor	Sq. Feet	% of Total	Cost
Paint Dept.			
Engine Dept.			
Totals			

Second Floor	Sq. Feet	% of Total	Cost
Window Dept.			
Electrical Dept.			
Accessory Dept.			
Totals			

OVERLAND CYCLE SHOP
Department Expense Allocation Spreadsheet
For Year Ended December 31, 2008

	Allocation Base	Account Balance	Allocation of Expenses to Departments			
			Adver-tising	Admin-istrative	Cycles	Clothing
Direct expenses						
Indirect utilities expense						
Total dept. expense						
Service dept. expenses:						
Advertising						
Administrative						
Total expenses allocated to operating depts.						

Supplemental expense allocation calculation:

Utilities expense:

	Square Feet	% of Total	Cost
Advertising			
Administrative			
Cycles			
Clothing			
Total			

Advertising expense:

	Ads Placed	% of Total	Cost
Cycles			
Clothing			
Total			

Administrative expense:

	Sales	% of Total	Cost
Cycles			
Clothing			
Total			

COZY BOOKSTORE Departmental Expense Allocation Spreadsheet For Period Ended _____							
			Allocation of Expenses to Departments				
	Allocation Base	Expense Account Balance	Adver-tising Dept.	Purchas-ing Dept.	Books Dept.	Magazine Dept.	News-paper Dept.
Total dept. expenses							
Service dept. expenses:							
Advertising........	Sales						
Purchasing......	Purchase Orders						
Total expenses allocated to operating depts...............							

Allocations of service department costs to operating departments

Advertising: _____

	Sales	% of Total	Cost
Books Dept.			
Magazines Dept.			
Newspapers Dept.			
Totals			

Purchasing: _____

	Purchase Orders	% of Total	Cost
Books Dept.			
Magazines Dept.			
Newspapers Dept.			
Totals			

Allocation of annual wages between two departments

	Hours Worked*	% of Total	Cost
Jewelry Dept.			
Hosiery Dept.			
Totals			

* Computation of hours worked in the two selling departments:

Jewelry department:

     Selling……………………………

     Arranging and stocking……….

Hosiery department:

     Selling……………………………

     Arranging and stocking……….

Total hours…………………………

Name _____

Definitely Included:

_____
_____
_____
_____
_____
_____
_____

Definitely Excluded:

_____
_____
_____
_____
_____
_____
_____

Neither Definitely Included nor Definitely Excluded:

_____
_____
_____
_____
_____
_____
_____
_____

(1)

Location	Net Income	Average Assets	Return on Assets
Location A			
Location B			

(2)

MEMORANDUM
TO:
FROM:
DATE:
SUBJECT: Investment analysis and recommendation

Preliminary calculations

Land Cost.......................

Improvements................

Total cost of lots............

Lots	Quantity	Price	Total
Canyon			
Hilltop			
Total Market value			

Allocated cost--value basis of allocation: _____

	Market Value	% of Total	Allocated Cost	Average Lot Cost
Canyon section				
Hilltop section				
Totals				

Chapter 21   Exercise 21-10[A]   *Name* _____

Preliminary calculations

Parts	Quantity	Price	Total
Lobster Tails			
Lobster Flakes			
Total market value			

_____

_____
_____

_____

Allocated cost (value basis allocation): _____

Parts	Market Value	% of Total	Allocated Cost	Cost per lb.
Lobster Tails				
Lobster Flakes				
Total				

(1) Cost of goods sold

Parts	Quantity	Cost	Total
Lobster Tails			
Lobster Flakes			
Total cost of goods sold			

(2) Cost of ending inventory

Parts	Quantity	Cost	Total
Lobster Tails			
Lobster Flakes			
Total inventory cost			

Average occupancy cost = _____

These costs are assigned to departments as follows:

Department	Square Footage	Rate	Total
_____ Dept.			
_____ Dept.			

Part 2

Value-based costs are allocated to departments In two steps:

(i) Compute market value for each floor space.

Floor	Square Footage	Value per Sq. Ft.	Total
_____ floor			
_____ floor			
_____ floor			
Total market value			

(ii) Allocate $_____ to each floor based on its percent of market value.

	Market Value	% of Total	Allocated Cost	Cost per Sq. Ft.
_____ floor				
_____ floor				
_____ floor				
Totals				

Usage-based costs allocation rate = _____

(i) Compute total allocation rates for the floors

Floor	Value	Usage	Total
_____ floor			
_____ floor			
_____ floor			

(ii) Rates are applied to allocate occupancy costs to department(s).

Department	Square Footage	Rate	Total
_____ Department			
_____ Department			

Part 3

Preferred Allocation Method _____

_____

_____

_____

_____

_____

_____

_____

Cost Center	Cost	Driver	Cost per Driver
Professional salaries			
Patient services and supplies*			
Building cost			

*Patient Services and Supplies will be Customer Supplies for P21-2B

Part 2 _____Service

Activity	Cost Driver	Cost per Driver Unit	Allocated Cost
Professional salaries	Hours		
Patient services and supplies*			
Building cost	Sq. ft.		
Total			
Average cost per patient (or customer for 21-2B)			

*Patient Services and Supplies will be Customer Supplies for P21-2B

_____Service

Activity	Cost Driver	Cost per Driver Unit	Allocated Cost
Professional salaries	Hours		
Patient services and supplies*			
Building cost	Sq. ft.		
Total			
Average cost per patient (or customer for 21-2B)			

*Patient Services and Supplies will be Customer Supplies for P21-2B

Analysis of Alternative Cost Allocation

_____

_____

_____

_____

_____

_____

_____

Problem 21-3A or 21-3B

				Combined
Forecasted Departmental Income Statements				
For Year Ended December 31, 2009				

<u>**Supporting computations:**</u>

_____

_____

_____

_____

_____

_____

_____

_____

_____

_____

_____

_____

_____

_____

_____

_____

_____

_____

_____

_____

_____

_____

_____

_____

_____

_____

_____

_____

_____

_____

_____

_____

_____

(a)

RESPONSIBILITY ACCOUNTING PERFORMANCE REPORT		
Manager, _____ Department		
For the _____		
	Budgeted Amount	Actual Amount	Over (Under) Budget
CONTROLLABLE COSTS			
Raw materials			
Employee wages			
Supplies used			
Depreciation--Equipment			
Totals			

(b)

RESPONSIBILITY ACCOUNTING PERFORMANCE REPORT		
Manager, _____ Department		
For the _____		
	Budgeted Amount	Actual Amount	Over (Under) Budget
CONTROLLABLE COSTS			
Raw materials			
Employee wages			
Supplies used			
Depreciation--Equipment			
Totals			

(c)

RESPONSIBILITY ACCOUNTING PERFORMANCE REPORT		
Manager, _____ Plant		
For the _____		
	Budgeted Amount	Actual Amount	Over (Under) Budget
CONTROLLABLE COSTS			
Dept. manager salaries			
Utilities			
Building rent			
Other office salaries			
Other office costs			
_____ department			
_____ department			
Totals			

Comparative Analysis of Manager Performance

_____

_____

_____

_____

_____

_____

_____

Problem 21-5A[A] or 21-5B[A]

Part 1

Allocation of joint costs on the basis of sales value

Cost Activity: _____

Grade	Sales Value	Percent of Total	Allocated Cost
No. 1			
No. 2			
No. 3			
Total			

Cost Activity: _____

Grade	Sales Value	Percent of Total	Allocated Cost
No. 1			
No. 2			
No. 3			
Total			

Cost Activity: _____

Grade	Sales Value	Percent of Total	Allocated Cost
No. 1			
No. 2			
No. 3			
Total			

	No. 1	No. 2	No. 3	Combined
Income Statement				
For Year Ended December 31, 2008				

Part 3

Analysis of Joint Cost

	Fiscal 2005	Fiscal 2004	Fiscal 2003
Total Revenue			
Home Office			
Entertainment Software			
Consumer Electronics			
Appliances			

Part 2

_____

_____

_____

_____

_____

_____

Part 3 Fast Forward

Total Revenue		
Home Office		
Entertainment Software		
Consumer Electronics		
Appliances		

Part 2

Importance of Comparable Responsibility Accounting Reports

_____
_____
_____
_____
_____
_____
_____
_____
_____

(1) Identification of any Ethical Concern(s)

_____
_____
_____
_____
_____
_____
_____
_____
_____
_____
_____

(2) Action Plan to Eliminate or Reduce any Ethical Concern(s)

_____
_____
_____
_____
_____
_____
_____
_____
_____
_____
_____
_____
_____

(3) Identification of Senior Security's Ethical Responsibility(ies)

_____
_____
_____
_____
_____
_____
_____
_____
_____
_____
_____

MEMORANDUM

TO:
FROM:
SUBJECT: Explanation of Home Office Expense in performance report
DATE:

<u>**Tutorial**</u>   <u>**Notes about Tutorial**</u>

(i) _____

_____

_____

_____

(ii) _____

_____

_____

_____

(iii) _____

_____

_____

_____

_____

MEMORANDUM

TO:

FROM:

SUBJECT: Applications useful in business and managerial decision making

DATE:

_____

_____

_____

_____

_____

_____

_____

_____

_____

_____

_____

_____

_____

_____

_____

_____

_____

_____

_____

Reasons for Increased Use of Activity-Based Costing

(1) _____
_____
_____
_____
_____
_____

(2) _____
_____
_____
_____
_____
_____

(3) _____
_____
_____
_____
_____
_____

(1) _____

_____

_____

_____

_____

_____

_____

_____

_____

(2) _____

_____

_____

_____

_____

_____

_____

_____

_____

_____

_____

_____

Hitting the Road--BTN 21-9

(1) Recommendation to the Segment Departments for Responsibility Reporting

_____

_____

_____

_____

_____

(2) Proposal for an Expense Allocation System

Expense	Allocation Base
Heat...........................	
Rent...........................	
Insurance..................	
Maintenance...............	

1. & 2.

Net sales growth (in percent)

Segment	Net sales percent change from 2003 to 2004
UK Retail....................................	
International Retail.......................	
Total..	

---

3. Identification of Fast-Growth Segment

_____

_____

_____

4. Identification of Most Profitable Segment

_____

_____

_____

5. Explanation of Management Use of Segment Information

_____

_____

_____

_____

_____

_____

_____

_____

(1) _____   (5) _____
(2) _____   (6) _____
(3) _____   (7) _____
(4) _____

Quick Study 22-2

Series	Cost behavior
(1)	
(2)	
(3)	
(4)	

Quick Study 22-3
(1) Estimated line of cost behavior:

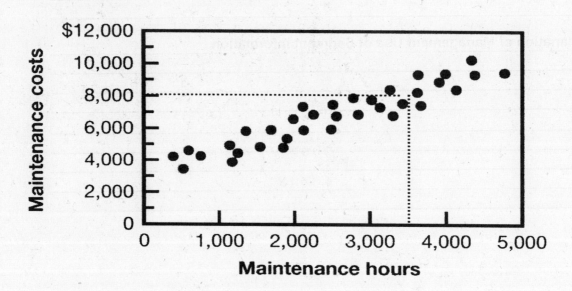

(2) Estimated cost components
Fixed costs: _____
_____

Variable costs: _____
_____
_____
_____

Variable Costs:

_____
_____

Fixed Costs:

_____
_____
_____
_____
_____

Quick Study 22-5

Contribution margin:

_____
_____

Contribution margin ratio:

_____
_____

Interpretation:

_____
_____
_____

(1)   Contribution margin per unit:

_____
_____
_____

(2)   Break-even point in units:

_____
_____
_____

Quick Study 22-7

(1)   Contribution margin ratio:

_____
_____

(2)   Break-even point in dollars:

_____
_____
_____

Quick Study 22-8

Units to be Sold to Yield Targeted Net Income

_____
_____
_____
_____
_____
_____

Quick Study 22-9

_____
_____

Identification of Company with Higher DOL: _____

Explanation: _____
_____
_____
_____
_____
_____
_____
_____

Quick Study 22-11

Number and Type of Beepers Sold at Break-even _____
_____
_____
_____
_____
_____
_____
_____
_____
_____

Exercise 22-1
Scatter diagram and estimated line of cost behavior.

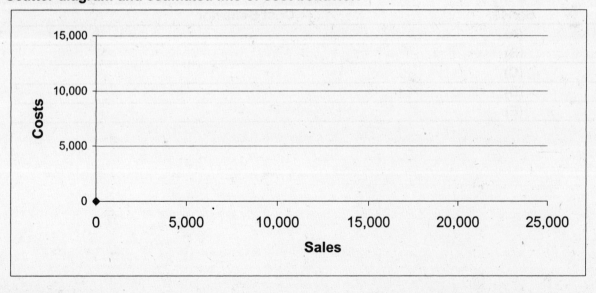

Cost behavior: _____
_____

Name _____

(1)

Graph	Cost Behavior
(1)	
(2)	
(3)	
(4)	
(5)	

(2)

Cost Item	Graph
(a)	
(b)	
(c)	
(d)	
(e)	

Exercise 22-3

(1)		(4)	
(2)		(5)	
(3)		(6)	

Exercise 22-4

Series	Cost Behavior
(A)	
(B)	
(C)	
(D)	
(E)	

Name _____

(1) Dollar Sales

_____

_____

_____

_____

_____

_____

(2) Total Variable Costs

_____

_____

_____

_____

_____

_____

Exercise 22-6

Scatter diagram and estimated line of cost behavior.

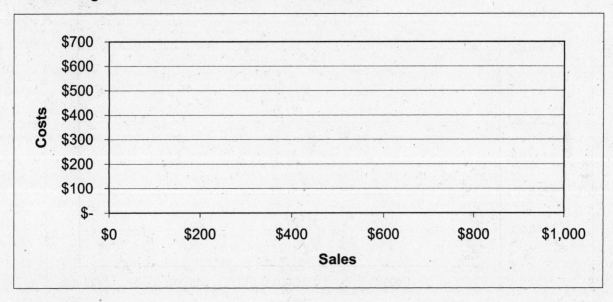

Cost behavior: _____

_____

(1)

(a)   Contribution margin per unit:

_____

_____

(b)   Contribution margin ratio:

_____

_____

(c)   Break-even point in units:

_____

_____

(d)   Break-even point in dollars:

_____

_____

(2) CVP chart:

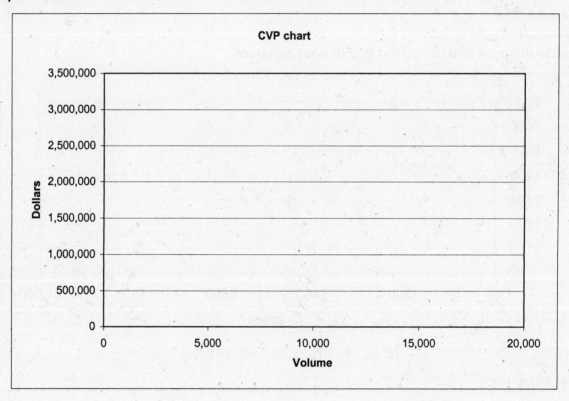

(1)

BLOOM COMPANY

Contribution Margin Income Statement (at Break-Even)

(2)

Sales (in dollars) to break even with increased fixed costs:

(1)   Unit sales at target income

_____

_____

_____

_____

_____

_____

_____

_____

_____

_____

(2)   Dollar sales at target income

_____

_____

_____

_____

_____

_____

_____

_____

_____

_____

Exercise 22-10

BLOOM COMPANY
Forecasted Contribution Margin Income Statement

_____

_____

_____

_____

_____

_____

_____

_____

(1) _____

_____

_____

_____

_____

(2) _____

_____

_____

_____

_____

_____

_____

_____

Exercise 22-12

1(a) Next Year's Total Expected Variable Costs _____

_____

_____

_____

_____

_____

_____

_____

1(b) Next Year's Total Expected Fixed Costs _____

_____

_____

_____

_____

(2) CVP Chart

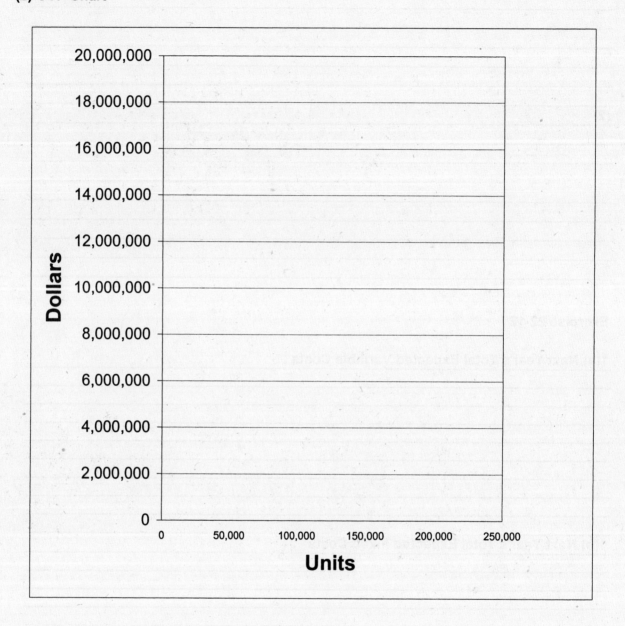

Company A's DOL:

_____

_____

_____

_____

_____

_____

_____

_____

_____

_____

_____

Company B's DOL:

_____

_____

_____

_____

_____

_____

_____

_____

_____

_____

_____

_____

_____

_____

Interpretation:

_____

_____

_____

_____

_____

_____

_____

(1) Selling price per composite unit:

_____
_____
_____
_____
_____
_____

(2) Variable costs per composite unit:

_____
_____
_____
_____
_____
_____
_____

(3) Break-even point in composite units:

_____
_____
_____
_____
_____
_____
_____
_____

(4) Unit sales of windows and doors at break-even point:

_____
_____
_____
_____

_____ Company **Contribution Margin Income Statement** For Year Ended _____	(_____ units)	Per unit	% of sales
Sales...			
Variable costs			
Contribution margin..			
Fixed costs			
Pretax Income..			
Income tax...			
Net Income..			

Part 3
Analysis

_____

_____

_____

_____

_____

_____

(a) Break-even point in unit sales:

_____
_____
_____
_____
_____
_____
_____
_____

(b) Break-even point in dollar sales:

_____
_____
_____
_____
_____
_____
_____
_____

Part 2
Graph for P22-2A

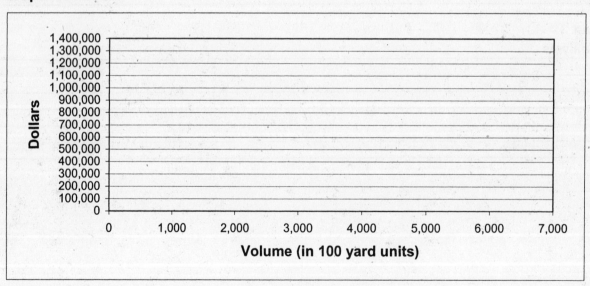

Graph for P22-2B

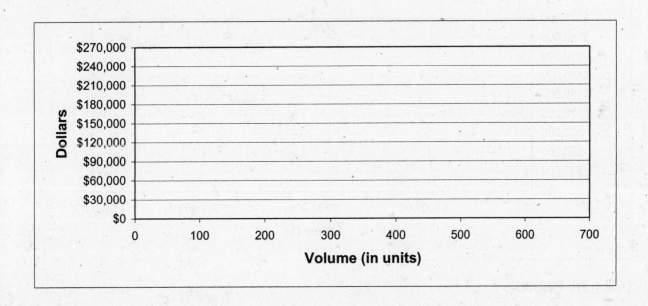

Part 3

Contribution Margin Income Statement (at Break-Even)	
Product_____	

Graph for P22-3A

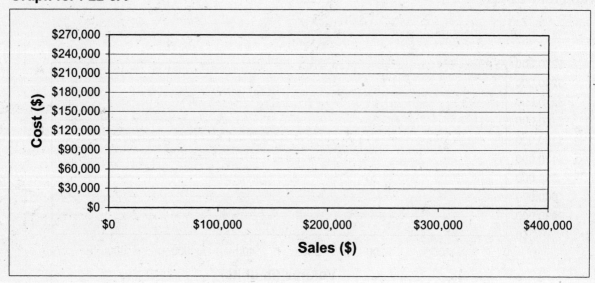

Graph for P22-3B

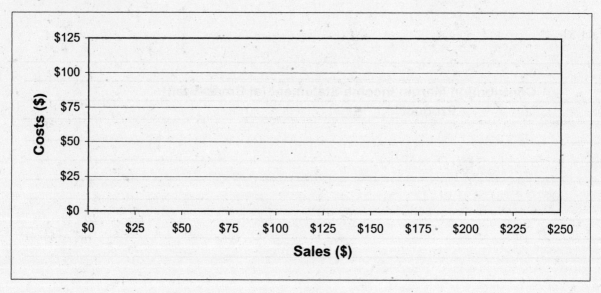

Variable costs per sales dollar: _____
_____
_____

Fixed costs: _____
_____
_____
_____

Part 3

	Predictions	
Sales (given)	$	$
Fixed costs (from part 2)		
Variable costs (from part 2)		
Total costs		

Year 2008 break-even in dollar sales:

_____
_____
_____
_____
_____
_____
_____
_____
_____
_____

Part 2

Year 2009 break-even in dollar sales:

_____
_____
_____
_____
_____
_____
_____
_____
_____
_____
_____
_____

Part 3

_____
_____

Forecasted Contribution Margin Income Statement
For Year Ended December 31, 2009

_____
_____
_____
_____
_____
_____
_____

Required sales in dollars:

_____
_____
_____
_____
_____
_____
_____
_____

Required sales in units:

_____
_____
_____
_____
_____
_____
_____
_____
_____
_____

Part 5

Forecasted Contribution Margin Income Statement
For Year Ended December 31, 2009

_____
_____
_____
_____
_____
_____
_____
_____

Break-even in dollar sales:

____ Product _____ :

_____

_____

_____

_____

_____

_____

_____

____ Product _____ :

_____

_____

_____

_____

_____

_____

_____

_____

_____

Part 2

_____ COMPANY Forecasted Contribution Margin Income Statement	Product _____	Product _____

_____ COMPANY		
Forecasted Contribution Margin Income Statement		
	Product _____	*Product* _____

Part 4

Identification and Explanation of Greatest Change in Product Income (Loss)

_____

_____

_____

_____

_____

_____

_____

Part 5

Description of Potential Factors Yielding Different Product Cost Structures

_____

_____

_____

_____

_____

_____

_____

(a) Plan 1's (Existing Strategy for 22-6B) break-even in dollar sales:

_____
_____
_____
_____
_____
_____
_____
_____

(b) Plan 2's (New Strategy for 22-6B) break-even in dollar sales:

_____
_____
_____
_____
_____
_____
_____
_____
_____

Part 2

_____COMPANY Forecasted Contribution Margin Income Statement	Plan 1 (Existing Strategy)	Plan 2 (New Strategy)

Break-even analysis assuming use of same materials:

Step 1: Compute break-even in composite units

_____

_____

_____

_____

_____

_____

_____

_____

_____

_____

_____

_____

Step 2: Compute break-even in individual product units sales

_____

_____

_____

_____

_____

_____

_____

Step 3: Compute break-even in individual product dollar sales

_____

_____

_____

_____

_____

_____

_____

Break-even analysis assuming use of <u>new</u> materials:

Step 1: Compute break-even in composite units

_____
_____
_____
_____
_____
_____
_____
_____
_____
_____
_____
_____
_____

Step 2: Compute break-even in individual product unit sales

_____
_____
_____
_____
_____
_____
_____

Step 3: Compute break-even in individual product dollar sales

_____
_____
_____
_____
_____
_____
_____

Part 3

Management Insight for Long-Term Planning

_____
_____
_____
_____

1. Selling price per composite unit

_____
_____
_____
_____
_____
_____

2. Variable costs per composite unit

_____
_____
_____
_____
_____
_____

3. Break-even point in composite units

_____
_____
_____
_____
_____
_____

4. Unit sales of desk units and chairs at break-even point

_____
_____
_____
_____
_____

(1) Identification of Costs _____

_____

_____

_____

_____

_____

_____

_____

_____

_____

_____

_____

(2) _____

_____

_____

_____

_____

_____

_____

_____

_____

_____

_____

_____

_____

(3) _____

_____

_____

_____

_____

_____

_____

_____

_____

_____

_____

_____

(1)

	Best Buy	Circuit City

(2) _____

_____

_____

_____

_____

_____

_____

_____

_____

_____

MEMORANDUM

To: "Mechanics" and "Owners"

From:

Re: Analysis of labor costs from survey data

Date:

REPORT ON REVENUE & COST ASSUMPTIONS

Revenue Assumptions:

Cost Assumptions:

Information and Resources Available for Entrepreneurs

_____

_____

_____

_____

_____

_____

_____

_____

_____

_____

_____

_____

_____

_____

_____

_____

_____

_____

_____

Questions for Completion of CVP Analysis

For School Administration:

For Business Owner:

_____

_____

_____

_____

_____

Part 2

_____

_____

_____

_____

_____

Part 3

_____

_____

_____

_____

_____

_____

_____

_____

(1) Types of information needed:

_____
_____
_____
_____
_____
_____
_____
_____
_____
_____
_____
_____
_____
_____
_____
_____
_____
_____
_____

(2) Useful tool(s) for analysis:

_____
_____
_____
_____
_____
_____
_____

(1) Potential Framework for Analysis

Product	Estimated Selling Price per unit	Estimated CM ratio	Estimated CM per unit	Estimated Sales Mix	Estimated CM for each component in composite unit

Total contribution margin (CM) per composite unit..................

_____

Estimated fixed costs per year: $_____

Break-even point in composite unit sales: $_____/$CM per composite unit =

Unit sales of individual products per year required to break-even: _____

_____

_____

_____

_____

_____

(2) Report on Results of Analysis from Part 1 (including break-even analysis)

_____
_____
_____
_____
_____
_____
_____
_____
_____
_____
_____
_____
_____
_____
_____
_____
_____
_____
_____
_____
_____
_____
_____
_____
_____

(1) Identification and Explanation of CVP Analysis

_____
_____
_____
_____
_____
_____

(2) Products Impact for CVP Analysis

_____
_____
_____
_____
_____
_____
_____
_____
_____
_____

(3) Store Impact for CVP Analysis

_____
_____
_____
_____
_____
_____

Necessary Component of Master Budget: _____

_____

Quick Study 23-2

(1) _____

(2) _____

(3) _____

_____

Quick Study 23-3

_____ Company
Computation of Budgeted Cost of Purchases
For Month Ended July 31

_____

_____

_____

_____

_____

_____

_____

Quick Study 23-4

(1) Comparative Analysis of Budgeting Approaches: _____

_____

_____

(2) Examples of Bottom-Up Budgeting: _____

_____

_____

_____

Computation of Budgeted Accounts Receivable Balance:

_____
_____
_____
_____
_____
_____
_____
_____
_____
_____

Quick Study 23-6

_____ Company
Cash Budget
For Month Ended March 31

_____
_____
_____
_____
_____
_____
_____
_____
_____
_____
_____
_____

Quick Study 23-7

(1) Description of Activity-Based Budgeting and Explanation of Budget Preparation

_____
_____
_____
_____

(2) Explanation of Differences between Activity-Based and Traditional Budgeting

_____
_____
_____

_____ Company
Production Budget
For Month Ended November 30

_____ Company Merchandise Purchases Budget For July, August and September	July	August	September

Supporting calculations:

_____
_____
_____
_____
_____
_____
_____
_____
_____
_____
_____
_____
_____
_____
_____
_____
_____
_____

(2) Ratio of Ending Inventory to Next Month's Sales for Each Budget Period

_____
_____

(3) Units Budgeted for Sale in October

_____
_____

_____ Company Cash Budget For January, February, and March	January	February	March

_____ Company
Cash Budget
For Month Ended July 31

_____

_____

_____

_____

_____

_____

_____

_____

_____

_____

_____

_____

_____

_____

Supporting calculations:

_____

_____

_____

_____

_____

_____

_____

_____

_____

_____

_____

_____

_____

_____

_____

		Company
	Budgeted Income Statement	
	For Month Ended July 31	

_____

_____

_____

_____

_____

_____

_____

_____

_____

_____

_____

_____

_____

_____

_____

_____

Supporting calculations:

_____

_____

_____

_____

_____

_____

_____

_____

_____

_____

_____

_____

_____

_____

_____

_____

_____

_____

_____

_____ Company
Budgeted Balance Sheet
July 31

Name _____

Merchandise purchases budgets

	August	September	October

Cash payments for purchases (on accounts) in October

	Dollars	Percent	Paid

Name _____

(1) Budgeted merchandise purchases:

	June	July	August

(2) Budgeted cost of goods sold:

	June	July	August

Exercise 23-7

(1) Budgeted merchandise purchases:

	July	August	September	October

Supporting calculations: _____

_____

_____

_____

_____

_____

_____

_____

_____

_____

Name _____

(2) Budgeted payments on accounts payable in September:

	Purchases	Percent Paid	Dollars Paid

Budgeted payments on accounts payable in October:

	Purchases	Percent Paid	Dollars Paid

(3) Budgeted balance of accounts payable at the end of September:

	Purchases	Percent Unpaid	Dollars Unpaid

Budgeted balance of accounts payable at the end of October:

	Purchases	Percent Unpaid	Dollars Unpaid

_____ Company		
Production Budget		
Second and Third Quarters		
	Second Quarter	Third Quarter

	Merchandise Purchases Budgets For Months of _____		
	Month of _____	Month of _____	Month of _____
Product: _____			
Product: _____			
Product: _____			

Identification and Explanation of Factors Yielding Fewer Purchases

_____

_____

_____

_____

_____

_____

_____

_____

_____

_____

_____

_____

_____

_____

_____

_____

_____

_____

	Cash Budgets For Months of _____		
	Month of _____	Month of _____	Month of _____

Supporting computations:

Cash collections of credit sales (accounts receivable)

From sales in month of:	Total	% Collected	Month of _____	Month of _____

Part 2

Budgeted ending inventories (in units)

	Month of _____	Month of _____	Month of _____	Month of _____

_____Company

Merchandise Purchases Budgets

For Months of _____

	Month of	Month of	Month of

Part 4

Cash payments on product purchases

From purchases in month of:	Total	% Paid	Month of	Month of

	Month of	Month of
Cash Budgets For Months of _____		

Part 6
Benefits to Management from Accurate Cash Budget Numbers

_____
_____
_____
_____
_____
_____
_____
_____
_____
_____
_____
_____

Part 1

	Budgeted Income Statements For Months of _____		
	Month of _____	Month of _____	Month of _____

Part 2: Recommendation on Implementation of Proposed Changes

Part 1

Month	Budgeted Units	Budgeted Unit Price	Budgeted Total Dollars

Part 2

	Month of	Month of	Month of	Total

Selling Expense Budgets

	Month of	Month of	Month of	Total

Part 3

| General and Administrative Expense Budgets | | | |
	Month of	Month of	Month of	Total

Supporting calculations:

Part 5

| Capital Expenditures Budgets | | | |
	Month of	Month of	Month of

	Cash Budgets		
	Month of	Month of	Month of

_____

Budgeted Income Statement
For Three Months Ended_____

_____
_____
_____
_____
_____
_____
_____
_____
_____
_____
_____
_____
_____
_____
_____
_____
_____
_____

Budgeted Balance sheet

_____
_____
_____
_____
_____
_____
_____
_____
_____
_____
_____
_____
_____
_____
_____
_____
_____
_____
_____
_____
_____
_____
_____
_____

Production Budget (in units)
_____ Quarter

Part 2

Direct Materials Budget (in lbs., except where noted)
_____ Quarter

SUCCESS SYSTEMS Budgeted Income Statements For Months of April, May and June			
	April	May	June

Part 2: Recommendation on Implementation of Proposed Changes

(a)
_____
_____
_____
_____
_____

(b)
_____
_____
_____
_____
_____
_____
_____
_____
_____

Part 2

(a)
_____
_____
_____
_____

(b)
_____
_____
_____
_____

Part 3

Fast Forward:
_____
_____
_____
_____
_____
_____
_____
_____

Computation of inventory reduction under new distribution system

Amount of ending inventory required at the 40% rule.... $ _____

Amount of ending inventory required at the 10% rule....   _____

Difference (inventory reduction)................................... $ _____

Implication of Distribution System for Inventory Level: _____

_____

_____

_____

_____

Part 2

Explanation and Justification of JIT Inventory System _____

_____

_____

_____

_____

_____

_____

_____

_____

_____

_____

_____

_____

_____

_____

Report on "Use It or Lose It" Budgeting

MEMORANDUM

TO: _____

FROM: _____

DATE: _____

SUBJECT: Concerns with sales staff input for the sales budget

Benefits of Using e-Budgets

_____
_____
_____
_____
_____
_____
_____
_____
_____
_____
_____
_____
_____
_____
_____

Part 2

Concerns with the Concept and Application of e-Budgets

_____
_____
_____
_____
_____
_____
_____
_____
_____
_____
_____
_____
_____
_____

College Costs Budget

_____
_____
_____
_____
_____
_____
_____
_____
_____

Part 1
Business Plan Elements

_____
_____
_____
_____
_____
_____
_____

Part 2
Benefits of Budgeting

_____
_____
_____
_____
_____
_____
_____

Hitting the Road--BTN 23-9

Part 1
Identification of External Factors When Setting Budgets

_____
_____
_____
_____

Part 2
Identification of Potential Factors Explaining Price Differences

_____
_____
_____
_____

Part 1
Importance of Administrative Expense Budget in Its Master Budgeting Process

_____

_____

_____

_____

_____

_____

_____

_____

Part 2
Identification of Administrative Expenses

_____

_____

_____

_____

_____

Part 3
Identification and Explanation of Person Responsible for Administrative Expense Budget

_____

_____

_____

_____

_____

	Company Flexible Budget Performance Report For Month Ended May 31		
	Flexible *Budget*	*Actual* *Results*	*Variances*

Quick Study 24-2

Actual Total Direct Labor Cost _____

Quick Study 24-3

Actual Total Direct Materials Cost _____

Actual Pounds of Materials Used _____

_____

_____

_____

_____

_____

_____

_____

_____

_____

_____

_____

_____

_____

Quick Study 24-5

(1) Description of Management by Exception Concept _____

_____

_____

_____

_____

(2) Explanation of How Standard Costs Aid Management by Exception _____

_____

_____

_____

_____

_____

Quick Study 24-6

Actual Total Overhead Cost _____

_____

_____

_____

_____

_____

_____

_____

GENERAL JOURNAL

Date	Account Titles and Explanation	P. R.	Debit	Credit

Quick Study 24-8

Sales	Actual	Flexible Budget	Fixed Budget
Units			
Price per unit			
Total dollars			

Name _____

	_____ Company			
	Flexible Budgets			
	For Quarter Ended March 31, 2008			
Flexible Budget		Flexible Budget for Unit Sales of _____	Flexible Budget for Unit Sales of _____	Flexible Budget for Unit Sales of _____
Variable Amount per Unit	Total Fixed Cost			

Item	Cost behavior
a. Depreciation on tools	
b. Pension cost	
c. Bike frames	
d. Screws for assembly	
e. Management salaries	
f. Incoming shipping expenses	
g. Office supplies	
h. Taxes on property	
i. Gas used for heating	
j. Direct labor	
k. Repair expense for tools	

Name _____

	Company		
Flexible Budget Performance Report			
For Month Ended June 30			
	Flexible	*Actual*	
	Budget	*Results*	*Variances*

_____
_____
_____
_____
_____
_____
_____
_____
_____
_____

Supporting calculations:
_____
_____
_____
_____
_____
_____
_____
_____
_____
_____
_____
_____
_____
_____
_____

_____ Company		
Flexible Budget Performance Report		
For Month Ended July 31		
Flexible Budget	*Actual Results*	*Variances*

Supporting calculations:

Chapter 24   Exercise 24-5

Part 1

October variances:

_____
_____
_____
_____
_____
_____
_____
_____
_____
_____
_____
_____
_____
_____
_____
_____
_____
_____
_____

Name _____

November variances:

_____
_____
_____
_____
_____
_____
_____
_____
_____
_____
_____
_____
_____
_____
_____
_____
_____
_____
_____

Interpretation of October Direct labor Variances

_____
_____
_____
_____
_____
_____
_____
_____

Exercise 24-6
Part 1
Predetermined overhead rate computations

_____
_____
_____
_____
_____
_____
_____
_____

Part 2
Variable overhead spending and efficiency variances:
   Computations:

_____
_____
_____
_____
_____
_____
_____

Interpretations:

_____
_____
_____
_____
_____
_____
_____
_____
_____

Part 3

Fixed overhead spending and volume variances

Computations:

_____
_____
_____
_____
_____
_____
_____
_____
_____
_____
_____
_____
_____
_____
_____
_____
_____
_____
_____

Interpretation:

_____
_____
_____
_____
_____
_____

Computation of Direct Materials Variances:

_____
_____
_____
_____
_____
_____
_____
_____
_____
_____
_____
_____
_____
_____
_____
_____
_____
_____
_____
_____
_____
_____
_____
_____
_____

Part 2

Interpretation of Direct Materials Variances:

_____
_____
_____
_____

GENERAL JOURNAL

Date		Account Titles and Explanation	P. R.	Debit	Credit

Part 2

GENERAL JOURNAL

Date		Account Titles and Explanation	P. R.	Debit	Credit

Part 3

Identification of Variance Investigated if Applying Management by Exception _____

_____

_____

_____

_____

_____

Computation of Total Overhead Variance

_____

_____

_____

_____

_____

_____

_____

_____

_____

_____

_____

_____

_____

_____

_____

_____

_____

_____

Part 2
Computation of Overhead Volume Variance

_____

_____

_____

_____

_____

_____

_____

_____

_____

_____

_____

_____

_____

_____

_____

_____

Computation of Overhead Controllable Variance

_____

_____

_____

_____

_____

_____

_____

_____

_____

_____

_____

_____

_____

_____

_____

_____

_____

(1) Computation of Sales Price and Sales Volume Variances

_____
_____
_____
_____
_____
_____
_____
_____
_____
_____
_____
_____
_____
_____
_____
_____
_____
_____
_____
_____

(2) Interpretation of Variances from Part 1

_____
_____
_____
_____
_____
_____

Direct Materials Cost Variances

Direct Labor Cost Variances

(a) Variable Overhead Spending and Efficiency Variances

(b) Fixed Overhead Spending and Volume Variances

_____
_____
_____
_____
_____
_____
_____
_____
_____
_____
_____
_____
_____
_____
_____
_____
_____
_____
_____
_____
_____
_____
_____
_____
_____
_____
_____
_____
_____
_____
_____

(c) Total Overhead Controllable Variance

_____
_____
_____
_____
_____
_____
_____
_____
_____
_____

Variable or Fixed Classification	Amount

	Flexible Budget		Flexible Budget for Unit Sales of _____	Flexible Budget for Unit Sales of _____
_____Company Flexible Budgets For Year Ended December 31, _____				
	Variable Amount per Unit	Total Fixed Cost		

Part 3
Operating income increase for a _____ to _____ unit sales increase:

Operating income (loss) at _____ units:

_____

_____

_____

_____

_____

_____

_____

_____

Problem 24-3A or 24-3B

Part 1

_____Company Flexible Budget Performance Report For Year Ended December 31, _____		
Flexible *Budget*	*Actual* *Results*	*Variances*

(a) Analysis of sales variance

	Total	Per Unit

Interpretation:

_____

_____

_____

_____

_____

(b) Analysis of direct materials variance

	Total	Per Unit

Interpretation:

_____

_____

_____

_____

Part 1

Variable or Fixed Classification	Amount
Variable costs (per unit):	
Fixed costs (per month):	

Part 2

_____ Company
Flexible Overhead Budgets
For Month Ended _____

Flexible Budget Variable Amount per Unit	Total Fixed Cost	Flexible Budget for Unit Sales of _____	Flexible Budget for Unit Sales of _____	Flexible Budget for Unit Sales of _____

Direct Materials Cost Variances

Direct Labor Cost Variances

_____

_____

_____

_____

_____

_____

_____

_____

_____

_____

_____

_____

_____

_____

_____

_____

_____

_____

_____

_____

_____

_____

_____

_____

_____

_____

_____

_____

_____

(a) Variable Overhead Spending and Efficiency Variances

(b) Fixed Overhead Spending and Volume Variances

_____

_____

_____

_____

_____

_____

_____

_____

_____

_____

_____

_____

_____

_____

_____

_____

_____

_____

_____

_____

_____

_____

_____

_____

_____

_____

_____

(c) Total Overhead Controllable Variance

_____

_____

_____

_____

_____

_____

_____

_____

_____

_____ Company

Overhead Variance Report

For Month Ended _____

Volume Variance

_____

_____

_____

_____

_____

Controllable Variance	Flexible Budget	Actual Results	Variances

Direct Materials Cost Variances

_____
_____
_____
_____
_____
_____
_____
_____
_____
_____
_____
_____
_____
_____
_____
_____
_____
_____
_____
_____
_____
_____
_____
_____
_____
_____
_____
_____
_____
_____
_____
_____
_____
_____
_____
_____
_____

Direct Labor Cost Variances

_____
_____
_____
_____
_____
_____
_____
_____
_____
_____
_____
_____
_____
_____
_____
_____
_____
_____
_____
_____
_____
_____
_____
_____
_____
_____
_____
_____
_____
_____
_____
_____
_____

(a) Variable Overhead Spending and Efficiency Variances

_____

_____

_____

_____

_____

_____

_____

_____

_____

_____

_____

_____

_____

_____

_____

_____

_____

_____

_____

_____

_____

_____

_____

_____

_____

_____

_____

_____

_____

(b) Fixed Overhead Spending and Volume Variances

_____

_____

_____

_____

_____

_____

_____

_____

_____

_____

_____

_____

_____

_____

_____

_____

_____

_____

_____

_____

_____

_____

_____

_____

(c) Total Overhead Controllable Variance

_____

_____

_____

_____

_____

_____

_____

_____

_____

| _____ Company |
| Overhead Variance Report |
| For Month Ended _____ |

Volume Variance

Controllable Variance	Flexible Budget	Actual Results	Variances

Part 1

GENERAL JOURNAL

Date	Account Titles and Explanation	P. R.	Debit	Credit

Part 2

Identification of Areas and Actions when Applying Management by Exception

_____

_____

_____

_____

_____

_____

_____

_____

_____

_____

_____

_____

SUCCESS SYSTEMS			
Flexible Budget Performance Report			
For Quarter Ended June 30			
	Flexible Budget	Actual Results	Variances
Desk Sales............................			
Chair Sales...........................			
Variable expenses..................			
Contribution margin...............			
Fixed expenses.....................			
Income from operations.........			

Supporting computations:

Identification of Foreign Currency Translation (FTC) Information

_____
_____
_____
_____

Part 2

Fiscal Year-End	F.C.T. Adjustment	F.C.T. Ending Balance
March 1, 2003		
February 28, 2004		
February 26, 2005		

Part 3--Fast Forward

(a) _____
_____
_____
_____

(b) _____
_____
_____
_____
_____
_____

	2 Years Prior	1 Year Prior	Current year	1 Year Ahead	2 Years Ahead
Best Buy					
Circuit City					

Part 2

Explanation of Sales Predictions

_____
_____
_____
_____
_____

Ethics Challenge--BTN 24-3

Specialty	Information Input and Explanation

MEMORANDUM

TO: _____

FROM: _____

DATE: _____

SUBJECT: Explanation and Implications of Favorable and Unfavorable Variances

Explanation of Benchmarking

_____

_____

_____

_____

_____

_____

_____

_____

_____

_____

_____

Part 2

Relation between Standard Costing and Benchmarking

_____

_____

_____

_____

_____

_____

_____

_____

_____

_____

Identification and Description of Time Elements Used for Competitive Advantage

_____
_____
_____
_____
_____
_____
_____
_____
_____
_____
_____
_____
_____
_____
_____
_____
_____
_____
_____
_____
_____
_____
_____
_____

Labor Variance Impacts from Worker Productivity _____
_____
_____
_____
_____
_____
_____

Part 2

Labor Variance Impacts from Labor Costs _____
_____
_____
_____
_____
_____
_____

Part 3

Joint Impact from Worker Productivity and Labor Costs _____
_____
_____
_____
_____
_____

MEMORANDUM

TO: _____

FROM: _____

DATE: _____

SUBJECT: **Explanation of Standard Costing and Variance Comments**

(1) Observe and Record the Number and Application of Raw Materials to Pizza

_____
_____
_____
_____
_____

(2) Identify and Record Differences Across the Two Businesses in Part 1

_____
_____
_____
_____
_____
_____

(3) Estimate and Explain which Business is More Profitable

_____
_____
_____
_____
_____
_____
_____
_____

Global Decision--BTN 24-10
(1)

Dixons	One Year Prior	Current Year	One Year Ahead	Two Years Ahead
Sales				

(2) Estimation and Explanation of Sales Predictions

_____
_____
_____
_____
_____

(1) Identification of Preferred Investment

_____
_____
_____

(2) Explanation of Why Investment B might be Preferred to Investment A

_____
_____
_____
_____
_____
_____
_____
_____

Quick Study 25-2

Payback Period

_____
_____
_____
_____
_____
_____

Quick Study 25-3

Net Present Value

_____
_____
_____
_____
_____
_____
_____
_____
_____
_____
_____

Accounting Rate of Return

_____
_____
_____
_____
_____
_____

Quick Study 25-5

Most Profitable Sales Mix

_____
_____
_____
_____
_____
_____
_____
_____
_____
_____

Quick Study 25-6

Incremental Cost Analysis

_____
_____
_____
_____
_____
_____
_____
_____
_____
_____

Year	Cash Flows	Present Value of 1 at 10%	Present value of cash flows	Cumulative present value of cash flows
0				
1				
2				
3				
4				
5				

Break-Even Time

_____

_____

_____

_____

Exercise 25-1

(a) Payback Period

_____

_____

_____

_____

_____

_____

_____

_____

(b) Payback Period

_____

_____

_____

_____

_____

_____

_____

_____

	Annual Net Cash flows	Cumulative Cash Flows
Year 1		
Year 2		
Year 3		
Year 4		
Year 5		

Payback Period

_____
_____
_____
_____
_____

Exercise 25-3

	Net Income	Depreciation	Net Cash Flow	Cumulative Cash Flow
Year 1				
Year 2				
Year 3				
Year 4				
Year 5				

Payback Period

_____
_____
_____
_____
_____
_____
_____
_____
_____

Accounting Rate of Return

_____
_____
_____
_____
_____
_____
_____

Exercise 25-5

	Net Income	Cash Flows
Sales		
Materials, labor & overhead		
Depreciation		
Selling and administrative		
Pretax income		
Income taxes		
Net income		
Net cash flows		

(1) Payback Period

_____
_____
_____
_____
_____
_____
_____

(2) Accounting Rate of Return

_____
_____
_____
_____
_____
_____
_____
_____
_____

	Annual Net Cash Flows	Present Value of Annuity at 8%	Present Value of Net Cash Flows
Years 1 through 6			
Amount invested			
Net present value of investment			

Acceptability of Investment _____

_____

_____

_____

Exercise 25-7

1.

Project C1

	Net Cash Flows	Present Value of 1 at 12%	Present Value of Net Cash Flows
Year 1			
Year 2			
Year 3			
Totals			
Amount invested			
Net present value			

Project C2

	Net Cash Flows	Present Value of 1 at 12%	Present Value of Net Cash Flows
Year 1			
Year 2			
Year 3			
Totals			
Amount invested			
Net present value			

	Net Cash Flows	Present Value of 1 at 12%	Present Value of Net Cash Flows
Year 1			
Year 2			
Year 3			
Totals			
Amount invested			
Net present value			

Analysis and interpretation:

_____

_____

_____

_____

2. Internal Rate of Return vs. 12% Net Present Value

_____

_____

_____

_____

3. Internal Rate of Return for C2

_____

_____

_____

_____

_____

_____

Exercise 25-8

	Normal Volume	Additional Volume	Combined Total
Sales			
Costs and expenses			
Direct materials			
Direct labor			
Overhead			
Selling expenses			
Administrative expenses			
Total costs and expenses			
Net income			

Management Recommendation:

_____
_____
_____
_____

Exercise 25-9

Incremental Cost of Making the Part:

_____
_____
_____
_____
_____
_____
_____
_____
_____

Incremental Cost of Buying the Part:

_____
_____
_____
_____
_____
_____
_____
_____
_____

Management Recommendation:

_____
_____
_____
_____
_____

Incremental Cost and Revenue of Additional Processing:

_____
_____
_____
_____
_____
_____
_____
_____
_____
_____
_____
_____
_____
_____
_____

Management Recommendation:

_____
_____
_____

Exercise 25-11

(1) No Departments Eliminated:

	Total	M	N	O	P	T
Sales						
Expenses						
Avoidable						
Unavoidable						
Total expenses						
Net Income (loss)						

_____
_____
_____
_____

(2) Departments with Expected Net Losses Eliminated:

	Total	M	N	O	P	T
Sales						
Expenses						
Avoidable						
Unavoidable						
Total expenses						
Net Income (loss)						

(3) Departments with Less Sales than Avoidable Expenses Eliminated:

	Total	M	N	O	P	T
Sales						
Expenses						
Avoidable						
Unavoidable						
Total expenses						
Net Income (loss)						

(1) Sales Mix Computations and Recommendation:

_____
_____
_____
_____
_____
_____
_____
_____
_____
_____
_____
_____
_____
_____

(2) Contribution Margin from the Recommended Sales Mix:

_____
_____
_____
_____
_____
_____
_____
_____

(1) Recovery time for:

    Payback Period _____

_____

_____

    Break-even Time _____

_____

_____

_____

(2) Advantages of Break-Even time _____

_____

_____

_____

_____

(3) Conditions Yielding Similar Results for Payback Period and Break-Even Time ____

_____

_____

_____

_____

Part 1

Annual Straight-Line Depreciation

_____
_____
_____
_____
_____
_____

Part 2

	Net Income	Net Cash Flow
Expected annual sales of new product		
Expected annual costs of new product		
Direct materials		
Direct labor		
Overhead excluding depr. on new asset		
Depreciation on new asset		
Selling and administrative expenses		
Income before taxes		
Income taxes		
Net income		
Net cash flow		

Computations:

_____
_____
_____
_____

Part 3

Payback period

_____
_____
_____
_____
_____
_____

Accounting rate of return _____

_____

_____

_____

_____

_____

_____

_____

_____

Part 5

	Net Cash Flows	Present Value of 1 at ____ %	Present Value of Net Cash Flows
Year 1			
Year 2			
Year 3			
Year 4*			
Totals			
Amount invested			
Net present value			

* Includes the salvage value impact.

_____

_____

_____

_____

Project _____ **Net Cash Flow** _____

_____

_____

_____

_____

_____

Project _____ **Net Cash Flow** _____

_____

_____

_____

_____

_____

_____

Part 2

Project _____ **Payback Period** _____

_____

_____

_____

_____

_____

Project _____ **Payback Period** _____

_____

_____

_____

_____

_____

Project _____ Accounting Rate of Return

_____

_____

_____

_____

_____

Project _____ Accounting Rate of Return

_____

_____

_____

_____

_____

_____

Part 4
Project _____ Present Value of Net Cash Flows

	Net Cash Flows	Present Value of Annuity of 1 at ____ %	Present Value of Net Cash Flows

Project _____ Present Value of Net Cash Flows

	Net Cash Flows	Present Value of Annuity of 1 at ____ %	Present Value of Net Cash Flows

Management Recommendation:

_____
_____
_____
_____
_____
_____
_____
_____

Problem 25-3A or 25-3B

Part 1 Results Using Straight-Line

	(a) Income Before Deprec.	(b) Straight-Line Deprec.	(c) Taxable Income (a) - (b)	(d) __% Income Taxes	(e) Net Cash Flows (a) - (d)
Year 1					
Year 2					
Year 3					
Year 4					
Year 5					
Year 6					

Part 2 Results Using MACRS

	(a) Income Before Deprec.	(b) MACRS Deprec.	(c) Taxable Income (a) - (b)	(d) __% Income Taxes	(e) Net Cash Flows (a) - (d)
Year 1					
Year 2					
Year 3					
Year 4					
Year 5					
Year 6					

Part 3 NPV Using Straight-Line

	Net Cash Flows	Present Value of 1 at ____%	Present Value of Net Cash Flows
Year 1			
Year 2			
Year 3			
Year 4			
Year 5			
Year 6			
Totals			
Amount invested			
Net present value			

Part 4 NPV Using MACRS

	Net Cash Flows	Present Value of 1 at ____%	Present Value of Net Cash Flows
Year 1			
Year 2			
Year 3			
Year 4			
Year 5			
Year 6			
Totals			
Amount invested			
Net present value			

Part 5

Explanation of MACRS Implications for NPV _____

_____

_____

_____

_____

_____

_____

_____

_____

Comparative Income Statement			
	(1) Normal Volume	(2) New Business	(3) Combined
Sales			
Costs and expenses			
Direct materials			
Direct labor			
Overhead			
Selling expenses			
Administrative expenses			
Total costs & expenses			
Operating income			

Supporting calculations:

_____

_____

_____

_____

_____

_____

_____

_____

_____

_____

_____

_____

_____

_____

_____

_____

_____

_____

_____

	Product____	Product ____
Selling price per unit		
Variable costs per unit		
Contribution margin per unit		
Machine hours to produce 1 unit		
Contribution per machine hour (or contribution/[hours per unit])		

Part 2

Sales Mix Recommendation: _____

_____

_____

_____

_____

_____

_____

_____

Contribution Margin at Recommended Sales Mix: _____

_____

_____

_____

_____

_____

Sales Mix Recommendation with Second Shift:

_____
_____
_____
_____
_____
_____
_____
_____
_____
_____
_____
_____
_____
_____
_____

Contribution Margin at Recommended Sales Mix:

_____
_____
_____
_____
_____
_____
_____
_____
_____
_____
_____

Management Decision:

_____
_____
_____
_____
_____
_____
_____
_____

Sales Mix Recommendation:

_____
_____
_____
_____
_____
_____
_____
_____
_____
_____
_____
_____
_____
_____
_____

Contribution Margin at Recommended Sales Mix:

_____
_____
_____
_____
_____
_____
_____
_____
_____
_____

Management Decision:

_____
_____
_____
_____
_____
_____
_____
_____

_____Company Analysis of Expenses under Elimination of Department_____	Total Expenses	Eliminated Expenses	Continuing Expenses
Cost of goods sold			
Direct expenses			
Advertising expense			
Store supplies used			
Depreciation of store equipment			
Allocated expenses			
Sales salaries			
Rent expense			
Bad debts expense			
Office salary expense			
Insurance expense			
Miscellaneous office expense			
Total expenses			

Supporting Computations: _____
_____
_____
_____
_____
_____
_____
_____

_____Company
Forecasted Annual Income Statement
Under Plan to Eliminate Department _____

_____
_____
_____
_____
_____
_____
_____
_____
_____
_____
_____
_____
_____
_____
_____
_____
_____
_____
_____
_____
_____
_____
_____

Part 3

_____Company
Reconciliation of Combined Income with Forecasted Income

Combined net income	$
Forecasted net income	$

Analysis and Recommendation: _____
_____
_____
_____

COMPUTING NET CASH FLOWS FROM NET INCOME

	Net income	Cash flows
Sales...	$ 300,000	$
Materials, labor, & overhead...............................	(160,000)	
Depreciation..	(40,000)	
Selling and administrative.................................	(30,000)	
Pretax income..	70,000	
Income taxes (30%)...	(21,000)	
Net income..	$ 49,000	
Net cash flows...		$

1. **Payback period** _____

_____

_____

_____

_____

_____

_____

_____

2. **Accounting rate of return** _____

_____

_____

_____

_____

_____

_____

_____

_____
_____
_____
_____
_____
_____
_____
_____
_____
_____
_____
_____

Part 2--Fast Forward
_____
_____
_____
_____
_____
_____

Identification and Cost of Advertising Space

_____
_____
_____
_____
_____
_____

Part 2
Estimation of Additional Product Sales to Cover Advertising Cost

_____
_____
_____
_____
_____
_____
_____
_____

Part 3

MEMORANDUM
TO:
FROM:
SUBJECT: Effective Advertising for Product Mix Decisions
DATE:

Part 1

Present Value Computation

_____

_____

_____

_____

_____

_____

_____

Part 2

Estimation Errors and Investment Project Evaluation

_____

_____

_____

_____

_____

_____

_____

_____

_____

_____

_____

MEMORANDUM

TO:

FROM:

DATE:

SUBJECT: Evaluating Capital Investment Opportunities

_____

_____

_____

_____

_____

_____

_____

_____

Part 2

_____

_____

_____

_____

_____

_____

_____

_____

_____

_____

Project Identification

_____
_____
_____
_____
_____
_____

Qualitative Factors in Management's Decision

_____
_____
_____
_____
_____
_____
_____
_____
_____
_____
_____
_____
_____
_____
_____
_____

(1) _____
_____
_____
_____
_____
_____
_____

(2) _____
_____
_____
_____
_____
_____
_____
_____

(1) Incremental Analysis:

	Model XR	Model CT

(2) Incremental Analysis:

	Model XR	Model CT

(3) Analysis and Recommendation:

_____
_____
_____

Hitting the Road--BTN 25-9
(1) Lease vs. Buy Decision:

_____
_____
_____
_____
_____
_____
_____
_____
_____
_____
_____
_____

(2) Management Recommendation to Lease or Buy

_____
_____
_____
_____
_____
_____

(1) Explanation of "Cost Activities"

_____
_____
_____
_____
_____
_____
_____

(2) Rationale of "Recycled Appliances" Program

_____
_____
_____
_____
_____
_____
_____

Appendix B   Quick Study B-1   *Name* _____

(1) _____

(2) _____

(3) _____

(4) _____

Quick Study B-2

Annual Rate of Interest _____

_____

_____

_____

Quick Study B-3

Years of Investment _____

_____

_____

_____

Quick Study B-4

Value of Investment _____

_____

_____

_____

Quick Study B-5

Cash Proceeds at Liquidation _____

_____

_____

_____

Quick Study B-6

Amount Willing to Pay for Project _____

_____

_____

_____

Appendix B   Quick Study B-7

Name _____

Future Value of Retirement Program

_____

_____

_____

_____

Exercise B-1

Years Until Payment

_____

_____

_____

_____

Exercise B-2

Rate of Interest to be Earned

_____

_____

_____

_____

Exercise B-3

Rate of Interest to be Earned

_____

_____

_____

_____

Exercise B-4

Number of Annual Payments to be Received

_____

_____

_____

_____

Exercise B-5

Rate of Interest to be Earned

_____

_____

_____

_____

Number of Annual Investments _____

_____

_____

_____

Exercise B-7

Cost (Present Value) of Automobile _____

_____

_____

_____

_____

_____

Exercise B-8

Cash Proceeds from Bond _____

_____

_____

_____

_____

_____

_____

_____

Exercise B-9

Present Value of Investment _____

_____

_____

_____

(1) _____
_____
_____

(2) _____
_____
_____

Exercise B-11

Amount Borrowed _____
_____
_____
_____
_____

Exercise B-12

	Single Future Payment	Number of Periods	Interest Rate	Table B.1 Value	Amount Borrowed
(a)					
(b)					
(c)					
(d)					
(e)					
(f)					

Appendix B   Exercise B-13   *Name* _____

(1) First Annuity: _____

_____

_____

_____

_____

_____

_____

_____

Second Annuity: _____

_____

_____

_____

_____

_____

_____

(2) First Annuity: _____

_____

_____

_____

Second Annuity: _____

_____

_____

_____

Exercise B-14

(1) Present Value of Annuity _____

_____

_____

(2) Present Value of Annuity _____

_____

_____

_____

(3) Present Value of Annuity _____

_____

_____

_____

Total Accumulated in the Account _____

_____

_____

_____

_____

Exercise B-16

Total Accumulated in the Account _____

_____

_____

_____

_____

_____

Exercise B-17

Future Value of the Fund _____

_____

_____

_____

Exercise B-18

Future Value of Investment _____

_____

_____

_____

Exercise B-19

	Present or Future Value	*Single Amount or Annuity*	*Relevant Table*	*Interest Rate*	*Number of Periods*
(a)					
(b)					
(c)					
(d)					

NOTES

NOTES

NOTES

NOTES

NOTES

NOTES